The New Cornish Garden

Tim Miles & David Rowe

Truran

Published by Truran 2003

Truran is an imprint of Truran Books Ltd Croft Prince, Mount Hawke, Truro, Cornwall TR4 8EE
www.truranbooks.co.uk

ISBN 1 85022 174 X

Printed and bound in Cornwall by R. Booth Ltd, Antron Hill, Mabe, Penryn, Cornwall TR10 9HH

Acknowledgements:
Douglas Adams, Chris Beausire, Ted Beausire, Mike Bell, Adrian Bonell, Mark Brent, Susan Butters, Carole Chapman, Roy Cheek, Maureen Clifford, Heather Corbett, Ivan Corbett, Frank Drinkwater, Lin Edgar, Jack Edwards, Falmouth Beach Hotel, Helena George, Alex Grant, Reggie Heyworth, Bob Hiscoke, Bruce Harnett, Marshall Hutchens, Graham Jeffrey, Roy Lancaster, Florence Lawrance, Neil Lucas, Clethra Matthews, Iain McHenry, Sharon McHenry, Membly Hall Hotel, Annie Miles, John Miles, Simon Miles, Wendy Miles, Sally Morris, Mike Nelhams, Jaimie Parsons, Steve Rayner, Kathy Rowe, Mike Rowe, Liz Selley, Philomena Selwood, Mike Sinnott, Nicky Smiljanovic, Candy Smit, Tim Smit, Jill Thomas, John Townsley, Helen Trelease, Roger Trenoweth, Mike Truscott, Reg Veevers, Miriam Wadey, Jan Wardle, Jono Wardle, Adrienne Wild, Peter Williams, Julie Wilson, Nick Wray

Also those departed authors and champions of Cornish gardening, W. Arnold-Forster (*Shrubs For The Milder Counties*), Don Hoyle (*Don Hoyle's Gardening Year in the South West*), and Edgar Thurston (*British & Foreign Trees And Shrubs in Cornwall*)

This book is dedicated to our children: Caitlin, Genevieve, Lamorna, Lydia and Rebecca

Contents

Foreword
Tim Smit

The names Trebah, Heligan, Trelissick, Lamorran, Glendurgan, Trewithen and Tresco trip off the tongue conveying an almost erotic frisson to the garden initiate. Anyone who loves horticulture will know that Cornwall's uniquely mild and moist climate caressed by the warming waters of the Gulf stream have created some of the finest man-made living theatres in the world. Indeed, millions come to visit our gardens and leave wanting to know more and those of us lucky enough to live here have long wanted to discover how to emulate these masterpieces in a domestic setting.

Oh how I could have used this marvellous book when I first rediscovered Heligan. The tantalising glimpses of exotica that poked through its undergrowth whetted my appetite and made my dreams take flight. However, my ignorance was total and as a result my dependence on others was complete. The intrepid plantsmen and botanists were well served with detailed tomes full of Latin which are full of foreboding to the amateur taking those first enthusiastic steps. There was nothing that could get you started, that captured the simple pleasure of trying things out filled with sensible tips on how to make these exotic treasures thrive...but now there is.

This is a wonderful book with excellent illustrations and, what is more, it is well written. Tim and David have done a "proper job" as they say in these parts. I've had the pleasure of knowing Tim for some ten years and can honestly say that he has forgotten more about these plants than most people will ever know. To journey with the authors on this practical odyssey is both hugely informative and gives even the least green-fingered among us a sense of hope that this time...

Enjoy.

One of the wonders of exotic Cornwall: the bizarre flower head of a giant rhubarb

Introduction
David Rowe

I can trace my own passion for the Cornish garden to a warm spring evening not long after I returned to Falmouth having spent too many years in a colder county and a friend asked: "What's the name of that tree?" It was my birthday, one of those landmark ages with a zero in it, and at the back of our house the large shrub garlanded with deep-red teardrop flowers was attracting more attention than the party host. I had to admit I didn't have a clue. It was pretty enough - beautiful even - but because I hadn't yet been bitten by the bug, I took little interest in the names of the plants around me. Luckily help was at hand in the form of another guest and old friend, Tim Miles, who just so happens to be a Royal Horticultural Society committee member and expert on Cornish planting. Instantly Tim identified it as mature *Crinodendron hookerianum*, not easy to say after a glass of wine. I preferred his less tongue-twisting name, Chilean lantern tree, which described it beautifully. This tickled my curiosity. How, I wondered after the party was over, did this plant – or at least its ancestors – get from the Andes to the Fal? Soon after the lanterns withered and fell, there was second magical burst of crimson from another corner of the garden. I did a little research of my own and found that this, too, was perfectly described by its common name, Australian bottlebrush, and that its forebears had first arrived from the New World more than 200 years ago. By now my friends had jokingly labelled my suburban jungle the Lost Gardens of Dracaena after the

A Chilean lantern tree in flower contrasts well with the bright new growths of *Pieris* 'Bert Chandler' (Clethra Matthews)

rather stunted pair of palm trees out the front. When I mentioned these to Tim he told me that they had their roots, so to speak, in New Zealand, and the Maoris even had a way of making porridge out of them. It helps having a world authority as a friend, especially when I found that Tim not only knew what these plants were, but also how they came to be here, too. As I cleared my garden, uncovering old shrubs and looking for new ones to put in, it dawned on me that I was living in the middle of a horticultural United Nations. I was gripped. Like so many before me, I had reached a certain age and my eyes were opened to the dazzling uniqueness of Cornish planting. Here I was in the garden capital of the world. It was revelation. More questions sprung like mushrooms. Why had I not taken in all this colour and shape in the past? Why were the hydrangeas in the back garden sky blue when the ones at the front were the cobalt-grey of a baby's eyes? Was this purple-

Introduction

flowered bush spilling over the granite wall the same as I'd seen on the cliffs of Treen while walking the coastal path? Not wishing to assail Tim with all this, I started to do more of my own research. Then I stumbled. I found many books on the glorious gardens of the far south-west but none which could tell me what I wanted to know about Cornwall's plants. What are their names? Where do they come from? What stories do they tell us? What conditions do they like? Why do plants from much warmer climes prosper here when we are nearer the Arctic than the equator? I wanted to find out the secrets of the Cornish garden but I wasn't sure where to turn.

As I delved deeper, I was reminded of something that I'd always known, that Cornwall is a maddening conundrum, a granite enigma wrapped in a warm sea. Stretching its toes into the buffeting Atlantic, the foot of Britain is a craggy place where thinly-scattered thorn trees are bent double by salt-laden southwesterlies. And yet, in the more

This congregation of spiky-leaved plants at Trebah is the essence of exotic Cornwall

sheltered parts, exotic trees can grow as tall as in their native lands. England's remotest county is largely deforested but has luxuriant gardens, which can be called subtropical. Blurry seasons and a relatively narrow temperature range mark the western land. You can be lightly tanned by the warm February sun or soaked and gale-blasted on the coastal path in August. Famously, those capricious skies can be grey and glued to the rooftops one-minute and Mediterranean blue the next, whatever day of the year. At Christmas, Cornwall is generally warmer than New York, and in summer, cooler and damper than Kent. The bleak heathlands have many more sheep than trees. And yet, in the woodlands of the south coast, there are still a few pockets of the temperate rainforest that once cloaked most of the county.

So what provides this mixture of bucketing-down rain, brilliant light, rare frosts and beguiling flora? How do the salty air and acid soils of a narrow peninsula more northerly than any of the United States of America except Alaska, sharing the same latitude as Kiev and Moose Jaw, Saskatchewan, sustain the flamboyant blooms of the Himalayas alongside the spiky desert succulents of Mexico and lilies of the veldt?

I soon learned from Tim that long before the Eden Project was even a slippery pit or the gardens of Heligan were lost, let alone found, mild, humid Cornwall was shipping in plants from around the globe, nurturing them, sheltering them, and claiming them as its own. It is now more than 300 years since the first camellia came in from Japan and 250 years since the first magnolia landed on

The glorious *Magnolia sargentiana robusta* (Roy Cheek)

East still splash the Cornish landscape with colour well over a century after they were first introduced. The wonderful legacy is that in the far south-west there are some of the finest gardens in the world, wild and tamed, new and ancient.

Having uncovered the gems of my own patch, I realised that the unique qualities of the Cornish garden are not just to be found in the famous magnolia-belt estates such as Trebah, Caerhays and Glendurgan or surrounding the great houses of Lanhydrock or Antony. In smaller town and village gardens, on roundabouts, along seafronts and in public parks, the heady spirit of botanical adventure thrives. The ingenious Cornish gardener is always trying something new. Today Japanese bamboo canes and Canary Island echiums grow as tall as bedroom windows. Banana plants flourish and agapanthus seem commoner than cabbages. Even in its roadsides, where many varieties of daffodil and daisy grow, Cornwall is like no other place. And in untamed nature, too, there is a captivating sense of the special. Go to the cliffs on a sunny May day and behold native plants and exotic immigrants. Gaze down on the thriving Hottentot fig, hebe, foxgloves and heather and you will see what looks like a domestic rockery on a biblical scale. These natural floral theatres were fashioned not by hand but by ice, sea, sun, wind and rain. How could any mortal compete with nature when the wild headland gardens of Cornwall have the Western Approaches washing up to them as the last word in water features?

the quayside from Virginia. About the same time Cornwall was being largely denuded of trees. Huge tracts of woodland were hacked down and turned into timber and fuel for mining and smelting. In the late 18th century, estate owners who garnered their fortune from the spoils of the earth made some effort to redress the balance by planting belts of trees to shelter their developing gardens. By the middle of the 19th century, plant hunting in India and the Himalayas was in full swing. Rhododendron seed brought back to Kew Gardens in London was dispatched down the railway line to estates such as Carclew and Heligan, where it was found that imported species often grew better in our peculiar climate than their own countries. Leading nurseries, most notably Veitch's of Exeter and Chelsea, sponsored new expeditions to China to satisfy the Victorian gentry's appetite for one-upmanship and the exotic. Today some of the original woodland plants which came back from the

As any gardener knows, and as Tim enlightened me, the biggest single natural factor in providing Cornwall with its temperate climate and long

Introduction

growing season is the Gulf Stream. Newfoundland is on the same latitude but temperatures there can be a good 12-15 degrees C lower in winter because it does not share the benefit of the warm water flow from the Caribbean. It has long been claimed, for example, that Madrid and Florence are no warmer in January than Penzance. By the time it crosses the ocean, the Gulf Stream should properly be called the North Atlantic Drift. Flowing at a sedate five miles per hour, it warms the 300-mile coastline of Cornwall and brings with it the gifts of early springs, long summers and short, mild winters. And, of course, that essential ingredient – rain, rain, rain. The south-westerly wind which drives the drift also chases in the wet from the Atlantic and scatters it on to Cornwall. A high average fall of 40-60 inches per year means moist soil, more cloud cover, fewer clear skies and consequently a reduced risk of severe cold. The first frosts of winter are often not until mid-

Cornish palms against a fine *Rhododendron arboreum* in full flower

December around Falmouth and Penzance. The Isles of Scilly are warmer still and in some winters remain frost-free. Even when a bitter wind does come from the east and north, Cornwall is protected partially by the landmass of the rest of Britain, and the salt air continues to take the edge off the cold. So I learned that Cornwall has to thank its southerly position and, most of all, the North Atlantic Drift, for bringing the rain, warming the land, and nurturing valleys of camellias and magnolias when more northerly parts of Britain are still waiting for crocuses to break through the snow.

Today Cornish gardening is entering a second golden age. The phenomenal success of the Eden Project is a fitting symbol for the renaissance of our famous gardens and the lasting inventiveness and skill of the Cornish gardener. It is a reminder that the prevailing beauty of this mercurial place lies in its river valleys, country lanes and coastal terraces, where you will find a range of plants as diverse as anywhere in the world.

Having established a few fundamentals about Cornwall, Tim and I decided to go further and write this book. We hope it will inspire. It is for those who love strolling through their favourite acres down here, who would like to know more about their own Cornish garden, or who want to recreate a pocket of the old county beyond the Tamar. We don't claim that it is anywhere near definitive. There is always so much more to see and learn in this elusive place. But in sharing some of the secrets of the Cornish garden, we have aimed to produce a valuable guide to recognising and growing some of the plants and flowers which make Cornwall so special.

Tim's Guide to Planting

Wind and shelter

No one who lives in or visits Cornwall needs reminding that it is a very gusty county. Fortunately, the prevailing southwesterlies are warmer than those less welcome blows from the north and east. Because of the general windiness, few native Cornish plants are tall growing. It wasn't until various wind-busting species were imported during the 19th century that it became possible to create year-round shelter for gardens and commercial crops. Two of the best evergreen hedging plants for Cornwall are *Olearia traversii* and *Quercus Ilex* (ilex oak). The former will reach two metres (seven feet) in two-three years, which makes it ideal for creating shelter quickly but it is frost tender. For long-term, frost-hardy shelter, ilex oak – which eventually grows up to nine metres (30 feet) – is preferable. Fast-growing, wind-resisting trees such as the Monterey pine and cypress can be used where greater height is required. These tend to shed their lower branches with age, so a lower-level planting (for example escallonia and/or elaeagnus) can be added to help prevent draughts. Ideally mix several different faster and slower growing types to create your shelter. Generally speaking, living natural wind resisters are more effective than walls or fences. Such solid barriers create severe turbulence on their leeward side, which can be even more damaging to plants than unfettered winds. Plastic mesh or traditional wooden slatted structures consisting of 50 per cent gaps are the most effective man-made filters.

Griselinias are valued for their leathery, salt-wind-resistant leaves. The cream-splashed foliage of *G. littoralis* 'Bantry Bay' are most prominent in winter

Aspect

To help you position various plants most effectively it is important to understand the impact of the aspect of your garden. Land which slopes to the north gets the least sun, particularly in winter, when it will remain cool, resulting in growth starting later, which often avoids frost damage. Land sloping east will get the morning sun. This can be detrimental in that it can stimulate plants into growth earlier, and when frost occurs on the flowers and young shoots the quick-thawing effect will damage them. West-sloping land will get the sun in the afternoon, when it is warmer, and into the evening, helping to maintain a higher temperature at night. Land sloping to the south is highly valued by gardeners as it gets sun for much of the day when it is at its hottest. It will also receive maximum available sunlight in winter. However, give careful thought before installing any shelter

This roundabout at the entrance to Falmouth leaves visitors in no doubt that they are entering a seriously exotic zone

planting, which may be required to check prevailing winds, in order to minimise shading of your prime site. An area of land near Penzance looking south towards St Michael's Mount became known as the Golden Mile because it produced the earliest crops in mainland Britain, commanding top prices until imported flowers and vegetables spoiled all that.

Frost pockets and microclimates

Imagine cold air being rather like water running in slow motion, flowing downhill until it can go no further. It gets trapped in hollows and as the temperature decreases at night, so these are the first places to freeze and they become frost pockets. This can be seen on a large scale in a valley or more localised if you have a dip in your garden. It is desirable to have a sloping garden that allows the cold air to run away. This is known as frost drainage. You should beware of obstructions such as walls, fences and hedges that could obstruct the flow. These should have gaps at ground level to allow the cold air to drain away. Wise gardeners work out which areas on their patch may be warmer or cooler than others. You may be able to locate favourable microclimates that can be used to grow the more tender plants which make Cornish gardening so special.

Sun and shade

Of the many wonderful plants of Cornwall, some require full sun and others shade from the sun. Your garden may already have various areas which can provide both. If not you can plant to provide shade for the future but avoid putting your valuable sunny corners into shade. It is usually possible to make an educated guess as to the natural habitat of a plant by its looks. Plants with large leaves such as *Rhododendron sinogrande* are designed by nature to collect as much light as possible. So it would be reasonable to assume that they would naturally grow in the shade of trees, and/or by streams, as they require plenty of moisture to support their large leaves. They are usually less tolerant of strong winds. At the other end of the scale, succulents such as agave have developed ways of reducing moisture loss through heat and wind by evolving thick, waxy-coated leaves and stems which can also store water. Such plants require a very sunny position and often resent moist soils. Of course there are variations to such general rules, but this principle should help you to understand your plants' needs and how to provide for them.

Soil

A vital part of growing most plants is the soil. Basically, a light, sandy soil is well drained but hungry in that it doesn't retain plant food well. Heavy clay soils are wet in winter and can crack and dry out in summer, but they tend to retain plant foods. Somewhere in between the two extremes is desirable for most plants. Organic material such as manure or garden compost will improve either type, helping to retain moisture in lighter soils and improve drainage and aeration in heavier ones. The pH level of a soil indicates its acidity or alkalinity. Seven is the neutral point on the scale – below is acid, above is alkaline. The vast majority of soils in Cornwall are acid, which is essential for growing rhododendrons. The pH of your soil can be adjusted, although it is easier to make a soil more alkaline than more acid. You can buy a simple testing kit to assess your own soil.

Wet soil around the base (where the top meets the roots) of some plants, particularly those from arid areas, is often fatal. Planting in a raised area and incorporating up to 80 per cent grit or coarse sand is greatly advantageous. Don't make the common mistake of digging a bigger hole for your plants and filling the bottom with grit before planting. Far from making the area dryer, it will act as a sump and draw water into it from the surrounding soil.

Plant nutrition

If there have been regular amounts of organic material going into the soil, your garden should be in good heart. Do make your own compost as it is very rewarding – traditionally the Cornish have even used freshly washed-up seaweed. Even leaf litter left to decompose in situ will over the years greatly contribute to your soil's well-being. Developing and maintaining a good soil organically should be a priority but chemical fertilisers can also have a part to play in Cornish gardening. A fertiliser high in nitrogen will encourage leaf growth which is useful in spring and summer. Phosphate is the second element usually carried in general fertilisers, of which most plants require just a small amount, though it can prove fatal to members of the protea family. The third principal component is potash, which encourages flowering and fruiting and also hardens the growth of shoots. A low nitrogen/high potash feed applied to frost-tender plants in late summer will improve their resilience – a liquid tomato feed is ideal. The content of

Like most members of this beautiful family, the sugar protea (*P. neriifolia*) resents the presence of phosphate in the soil (see plant nutrition, above)

Arid scapes like this at Mousehole will greatly benefit from the addition of drainage-enhancing material such as coarse grit or pea shingle before planting (see soil p 11)

fertilisers is indicated by the ratio of nitrogen, phosphate and potash (N.P.K. are their chemical symbols). Fertilisers are applied in liquid, granule or powder form. Liquid is the quickest acting. Applying more than the recommended amount of any fertilizer is usually a waste of money.

Mulch

Mulch is basically a material used to create a layer on top of the soil. Depending on the material used, it can retain soil moisture, suppress weed growth and/or insulate the soil and the plant root systems underneath. A mulch can also enhance the appearance of plants, for example arid plants look better when mulched with grit or shingle, whereas bark or leaf litter look better in a woodland environment.

Planting

In an ideal world it is preferable to plant in spring when the worst of the frost and wind has passed. This allows plants to have the maximum establishing time before their first Cornish winter. But don't fall into the trap, as many do, of purchasing all your plants in full flower in spring. Irresistible as they are, you will end up with a predominantly spring-flowering garden with little to follow. We aim to encourage you to consider your garden as year-round entertainment and take full advantage of the range of plants which will grow.

Winter frost protection

This can be achieved much more easily now with horticultural fleece. It is simple, clean and tidy to use, easy to store, and will last several years. It can be over-conspicuous in the landscape but an outer layer of hessian will give a more rustic finish. Fleece can be applied in a number of layers to increase its effectiveness. Plants can be wrapped easily when cold weather threatens, while de-fleecing is a simple matter when the danger is passed. Remember that frost most readily strikes when there is no cloud cover to retain the warmth generated by the sun during the day.

Choosing and using plants

Many volumes have been written on garden

design, and as an art form gardening is of course very subjective. A good basic rule is to consider the associations between plants, and which ones you want to group together for best effect.

For example, arid-looking plants such as agave and jungly plants like banana send different images and can look incongruous together. It's probably better to have a separate theme of one or the other, or have both if you wish in separate areas of the same garden. Also consider combining plants which set one another off. For example, the spreading style of gunnera looks well with a tall bamboo, their habit of growth and extremely different-sized leaves contrast superbly. It is wise to create a balance between exuberant tender plants and a backbone of staunch 'good doers' in case of the occasional harsh winter.

Give it a go

The great gardens of Cornwall have developed from a philosophy simply summed up as "give it a go." Over the last two centuries thousands of plants have been tried here. Many will not have survived their first winter while many others will have perished in their first hard winter. Maybe they weren't big enough to be tough enough. Maybe they were planted in a less-than-ideal spot. Whatever, many will probably have been replanted in a different garden at a later date and have thrived, at least for a time.

A favourite exotic plant of mine is *Lonicera hildebrandiana*, the giant honeysuckle from Burma. This is not particularly cold hardy but during mild years it will flourish in sheltered gardens,

scrambling vigorously, producing huge white and yellow sweetly scented florets quite wonderfully. If killed by a cold spell it is difficult to replace, as it is not widely available. Because of this it is not often seen but it is well worth seeking out.

Cornish gardening at its best includes the propagation of tenderish plants as potential replacements after a hard winter. Should the parent plants survive the coldest months in the garden, giving away or swapping your excess stocks can make new friends. Everyone will be richer for the experience – and New Cornish Gardening will go from strength to strength.

The late George Sowden, long-serving head gardener at Fox Rosehill, Falmouth, with the Japanese banana tree which so inspired Tim as a youngster

Magnolia

The beautiful *Magnolia stellata* is free-flowering from an early age. Its modest stature and durability make it well suited to the smaller plot

If there were ever such a thing as a Miss World contest for garden plants, the magnolias of Cornwall would surely take the crown. The early spring profusion of goblet-shaped flowers, some opening up to the size of dinner plates, ranging in colour from shocking pink to white, has the power to render the onlooker speechless in wonderment. Caerhays holds the national collection of these superlative trees and shrubs from Asia and the Americas and there is no better place to see them. Lanhydrock, too, is a great magnolia stronghold.

Generally speaking, the most impressive magnolias are early flowering and therefore susceptible to frost spoiling the blossom, so the sheltered Cornish woodland gardens are the perfect places to grow them. One of the earliest to flower (in February) is *Magnolia campbellii,* also known as the pink tulip tree, a native of the Himalayas. Our old friend Edgar Thurston notes a fine 12 metres (40 feet) specimen at Bosahan, planted in 1888. By 1921 it had an amazing 500 blooms. Not many of us, though, have the ideal conditions for such graceful giants, or come to that, the time to count the flowers! Most of the other huge-flowered types such as *M. sargentiana, M. sprengeri diva*, and a Cornish hybrid of these two *M.* 'Caerhays Belle', bloom more or less together in March, creating amazing spectacles. *M.* 'Star Wars' is a superb smaller-growing version of the established Cornish giants, flowering early in life over an extended period. It is a good choice for Up Country and smaller gardens. If hit by frosts, it will still produce more flowers, whereas the others tend to have a single flush of blooms.

The breathtaking sight of massed, early-flowering magnolias at Lanhydrock

M. stellata from Japan is one of several good choices for smaller gardens and large pots. Its fragrant, star-like white flowers open during March and April in profusion. It is a compact grower, eventually reaching three metres (ten feet). A form to look for is 'Royal Star', which flowers later and so has more chance of avoiding frosts. Another name to seek out is a hybrid of stellata called *M. x loebneri*. Two forms of this, 'Leonard Messel', which has a lilac pink flower, and 'Merrill' (white) are very tough and suitable for most soil types, including chalky. Each will make a large shrub or small tree and is tolerant of some exposure.

Over the years magnolia breeders have shown great patience as it can take up to two decades for a new seedling to flower. Buy plants that have been grafted or grown from cuttings and these will flower earlier in life.

The huge bloom of *M. sargentiana robusta* – arguably the most admired and extraordinary of all the Cornish magnolias

15

Camellia

The simple beauty of Cornish favourite *Camellia x williamsii* 'St Ewe' is quite a contrast to the blowzy double-flowered types

There are so many varieties of these evergreen trees and shrubs known for their luxuriant blooms and lustrous foliage, it was difficult to decide which to feature. We settled upon the single-flowered *Camellia* 'St Ewe' (*Camellia x williamsii* 'St Ewe') because it was created at one of the great beauty spots of Cornwall, Caerhays Castle, and named after a tranquil village nearby. Its creator John Charles Williams was head of a family whose considerable wealth came from the Cornish mining industry. JCW was a great supporter of the celebrated plant hunters who travelled the world to gather and send back new species. *C.* 'St Ewe' was conceived in the 1920s when he crossed two natives of China and Japan, *C.saluenensis* and *C. japonica*, to make a deep-pink, cup-shaped flower which often blooms from November to May.

The vicar tells us there is a particularly fine example of this lovely plant by the war memorial in St Ewe churchyard. Aficionados of the Lost Gardens of Heligan, which lay just within the boundaries of the parish, will be familiar with this monument. Poignantly, many names featured on it also appear on Heligan's lavatory walls, written just before the gardeners went off to the First World War. Most never came back.

Considered the queens of spring-flowering shrubs, camellias form the backbone of most Cornish gardens. They generally grow to around two metres (seven feet) in height but vary between types, and some can become tree-like in time. Some 100-year-old specimens reach as high as ten metres (33 feet). They prefer an acid soil, which is moisture-retentive but does not become

Consider planting white varieties to provide a contrast with the widely grown pinks and reds

waterlogged. Dry soil, particularly in July and August, will result in a lack of flower bud formation for the following season's display. A camellia's compact, fibrous root system makes it well suited to pot growing and the plant is a cheerful addition to a cool conservatory in winter. When planting outdoors, avoid positioning in the early morning sun, as it will damage open, frosted flowers. Camellias can be pruned or even clipped tightly immediately after flowering, leaving time during the summer for next season's buds to form. The rich green leaves make camellias an excellent backdrop for summer flowers and a strong winter feature when deciduous shrubs and trees have lost their leaves and perennials have died back. They provide important shelter for many more tender plants in Cornish gardens. A woodland site with light overhead shade is ideal – yet they often flower more freely in full sun so long as the soil doesn't dry out in summer.

The williamsii types make an excellent evergreen flowering hedge. They are also gardener-friendly, shedding their unsightly old bloom naturally, sparing us the laborious task of deadheading by hand

Rhododendron & Azalea

Spring in Cornwall is famed for its glorious riot of rhododendron flower. There are many types to choose from, so with careful selection even the smaller garden can display rhodo blossom for weeks on end

Countless volumes have been dedicated to the stately rhododendron, so we have to confess it is difficult to do it justice in so few words. There are more than 800 species, mostly from the mountainous regions of China, Tibet and Burma, some of which thrive in cooler areas of Britain. It is fair to say that Cornwall has had a major part to play in the history of 'rhodos'. Most grow better here than in their native soils and in turn they have become the most widely seen ornamental plants in our great gardens. They vary from tiny rockery plants to magnificent large-leaved trees, all providing wonderful displays of blossom. The bigger types such as *R. sinogrande* produce individual leaves up to a metre (three feet) long, and thrive in the valley gardens of Cornwall, where they are sheltered from hot sun and strong winds. These giants aside, most types enjoy having their tops in sunshine and have varying degrees of tolerance to winds. Add to this the county's higher than average rainfall and predominance of acid soil and the conditions are near perfect.

An early frontrunner was *R. arboreum*, which soon established itself as the backbone of Cornish gardens after being introduced in 1810. During Victorian times many more species arrived, leading to much hybridising and a plethora of new varieties which often proved tougher and even more beautiful than the originals. Samuel Smith, head gardener at Penjerrick for 46 years until 1935, was particularly successful and his *R.* 'Penjerrick' is widely considered the finest hybrid ever raised. Another choice hybrid is *R.* 'Sir Charles Lemon', named after the creator of Carclew and sponsor of some of the first seed-gathering expeditions. Other

Scientifically, azaleas have become known as rhododendrons. This deciduous type is now *R. luteum* and is widely enjoyed in Cornish gardens for its fragrant flowers in May, followed by a blaze of rich leaf tints in autumn

rhododendrons have local names such as 'Cornish Cross', 'Barclayi Robert Fox' and 'Beauty of Tremough'. So many of the county's gardens have magnificent displays. Tim's favourites are Trelissick, Caerhays, Trengwainton and Trewithen.

The flowering season runs from December to August with most types performing during March to May. There is a vast range of colour, but even while out of flower their luscious leaves and warm-toned barks make them very attractive.

Azaleas, now officially known as rhododendrons, are generally of modest stature with smaller flowers en masse, often smothering the whole plant. Happily, like their big sisters, they tend to be trouble free. There is a huge choice of 'rhodos' and it is well worth studying specialist books and nursery catalogues before making your own selection. Many are small enough for a modest-sized garden or for keeping in containers. Either way, never let them dry out. The hardy hybrids are very tough and can be grown Up Country. It is important to remember that most types resent cold winds.

Often seen as a tree, *R. arboreum* is one of the noblest of this huge family. Another big grower is *R. ponticum*, which can be a thug, but is highly valued as a windbreak

Pieris

Spring in Cornwall would be much the poorer without the refined beauty of the pieris

The name of this unsung star derives from the Pierides, also known as the Muses, those inspirational nymphs of mythology. It is an apt one for a slow-growing evergreen from China and Japan which has delighted many a Cornish gardener. Prominent flower buds are formed in autumn, exhibiting throughout winter the great promise of things to come. In some types these buds are attractively tinged red. Come early spring, they develop into enchanting panicles of lily-of-the-valley type flowers. At first this a solo performance, soon turning into a duet with the plant's coloured young leaves.

There are a number of different forms. Some are geographical variations found in the wild, while breeding in gardens has created others. These include types with pink flowers and some with a creamy-white leaf variegation. A popular and lovely variety is *Pieris* 'Wakehurst', which takes its name from Wakehurst Place, the well-known satellite of the Royal Botanic Gardens Kew. Sadly, like many types, its vivid red new leaves are prone to frost damage. However, a hybrid called *P.* 'Forest Flame', produced from 'Wakehurst' and the tougher japonica, has inherited the wonderful young leaf colour, yet is more tolerant of frosts. Its leaves emerge red, change to pink, then creamy yellow, and finally to green, while the white flowers appear in large drooping panicles. A variegated form of japonica called 'Flaming Star' is slower growing, but is also very desirable. Another variety, 'Charles Michael', named after a long-serving head gardener at Caerhays who retired in the 1950s, is an excellent choice for milder counties. It has the largest individual flowers of any pieris and should

Although the coppery-red young growths of *P. japonica* are not the most striking of the group, this favourite displays its flowers in great abundance

P. forrestii is an outstandingly beautiful shrub, combining masses of white flowers with brilliant red new growths (Clethra Matthews)

be more widely grown. *P.* 'Bert Chandler' (see p 5) is a shy flowering variety raised in Australia, and valued for its range of foliage effects through the seasons. Because so many Cornish gardens usually miss the damaging late frosts, a whole range can be seen here in their full splendour.

Pieris are of the same family as rhododendron, and therefore require an acid soil which doesn't dry out. They are usually seen at their best grown in light woodland, where they enjoy the cool, moist soil, and shade from the hottest sun. They are best positioned where they are not in visual competition with flamboyant companions such as rhododendron and camellia, otherwise their more subtle beauty can be overshadowed. For the patio they make good container plants, but benefit from a cooler position during the warmest months, together with constant soil moisture. A bark mulch on the pot will help maintain this. Prune out straggly, weak or dead growth to keep your pieris looking smart.

Chilean Lantern Tree

Crinodendron hookerianum may be a bit of a mouthful, but imagine asking for a *Tricuspidaria lanceolata* down at the garden centre! These are the current and former names of this South American treasure, a shrub or small tree which would figure in many a West Country gardener's top ten.

Dripping with flowers, the Chilean lantern tree (*Crinodendron hookerianum*) is one of Cornwall's great floral delights

As the common name suggests, it is a native of the forests of Chile, and also of the off-island of Chiloe. It was introduced here in 1848 by the Cornish plant-hunter William Lobb for Veitch's nursery of Exeter and quickly established itself as a great favourite. Edgar Thurston reported in 1930 that there were some fine examples dotted around the county, in particular "at Burncoose (27ft. high); Penjerrick (25ft.); Carclew (20ft. high, spread 16ft. 6in)." Tim even heard of an 80-yard hedge at Caerhays, planted as a windbreak. The head gardener Jaimie Parsons tells us this was so, though some trees were blown out in the hurricane of 1990 and parts of the hedge had to be replanted. This large evergreen is in its glory in May-June when its 2.5 cm (1 inch) crimson "lanterns" appear suspended on long stalks. Unusually, these stalks are formed during the previous autumn and hang attractively all winter with the tiny flower bud at the tip. The combination of the peel-like petals of the flowers and the narrow, dark-green leaves gives an enchanting effect in the evening light. Some romantics (including Tim) claim that the lanterns even appear to glow.

The Chilean lantern tree is hardy in most Cornish winters. It is occasionally cut back during a hard winter but will usually regenerate from the older wood. In colder areas, plant in sheltered sites,

The dark matt foliage of the lantern tree makes it a wonderful backdrop for many other flowers, as well as its own

avoiding chilly winds and frost pockets as well as hot, dry positions. Being a forest-dweller, it enjoys having its roots in the shade and a moist – but not wet – soil. It will flower merrily with its top in full sun or light shade. Given its origins, it is surprisingly wind-tolerant, but avoid exposing it to cold northerlies, easterlies and full sea blasts. It is suitable for planting as a hedge or screen which can be trimmed, ideally immediately after flowering. Expect a growth rate of about a metre (three feet) every five years.

These gorgeous lanterns look almost good enough to eat

Chilean Fire Tree

Choose your own superlatives to describe this adopted Cornish treasure. The Chilean fire tree (embothrium) is one of many South American plants which thrive in our gardens

We're going to stick our necks out here and say that this plant gives the most brilliant display of colour of any tree grown outdoors in Britain. It's a member of the diverse protea family, which takes its name from the Greek god Proteus, who could change himself into many shapes. There are many proteas but few can match this spectacular tree which hails from Chile and southern Argentina, where it is found on the coasts and in the Andes. In Chile, we are told, the leaf is traditionally used to ease toothaches and headaches, though we can't vouch for such remedies. The embothrium, to give the fire tree its proper name, was first introduced to Britain in 1846 by William Lobb. Today it thrives in Cornwall and Ireland, where the moist air must remind it of the mountain mists of its homelands. Indeed, it has been known to grow up to 15 metres (50 feet) here, bigger than in the wild. We know of fine specimens at Trelissick, Fox Rosehill and Trewithen, all of which give stunning displays during late spring and early summer. Because the plant is so widely distributed in its native lands, it is variable in flower colour, leaf shape and hardiness. We have chosen to feature two types because of their hardiness, superior foliage and flower power. *E. longifolium* has brilliant scarlet flowers along its branches and tends to be evergreen. The semi-evergreen *E. lanceolatum* is perhaps the hardiest type and the 'Norquinco' form, in particular, with its profusion of orange-scarlet flowers, is well worth seeking out. The flowers of all types look wonderful in the evening light.

The embothrium requires a lime-free soil, moisture-retentive but not heavy. Dig in plenty of organic matter such as peat or leaf-mould before planting, and mulch annually, as this helps preserve water in the soil during summer.

It is important to use a phosphate-free fertiliser with all members of the protea family as too much phosphate can kill them off. Positioned away from drying winds, the embothrium is seen at its best in an open woodland setting, although the 'Norquinco' seems tolerant of more exposed sites if given a shaded root run to prevent the soil drying out.

Fire trees are seen at their best in an open woodland setting, although some forms are more wind tolerant than is often realised

Blossom colour varies from scarlet to striking orange. Yellow and white forms have also been seen in the Andes

Hydrangea

The charming flowerheads of the lacecap hydrangeas lend a refined air to the summer garden

The fickle nature of garden fashion means that this great stalwart of the Cornish scene is often dismissed or just taken for granted. This is unfair on a plant which is perfect for our climate, needs little attention, and provides a colourful display long after the primadonnas of spring such as camellias and magnolias have shed their last petals. Hydrangea takes its name from the Greek words hydor (water) and aggeion (vessel), referring to its cup-shaped seed capsules. Most of the 23 species will grow in Cornwall but *H. macrophylla* from Japan is the most durable and widely seen. This is a species of great variation, divided into two distinct types – mopheads (more sophisticatedly known as hortensias) and lacecaps, after the shape of the flower clusters. Tim was put off hydrangeas when younger by the coarse appearance of the mopheads, the commonest type in Cornwall. He is now a big fan of lacecaps, largely due to the enthusiasm of Barry Champion, head gardener at Trelissick, who has developed an impressive collection.

In a sheltered garden with dappled shade, hydrangeas will grow up to three metres (ten feet). They are also tolerant of exposed positions close to the sea. where 1.8 metres (six feet) is the maximum expected height. They are happy in full sun but resent being dry at the roots. Even though they are deciduous, their twiggy growth and old flowerheads (considered by many to be attractive features) act as filters to the winter wind, making them effective shelter providers. Flower colour is dramatically affected by the pH of the soil, causing blues to turn pink on alkaline soils. Whites are less susceptible to this phenomenom. Your soil or pot-

The mophead types are a most valuable element of the Cornish scene. As well as encouraging more flowers, dead-heading fading blooms keeps up appearances - and makes the photographer's life easier!

A selection of hydrangeas at Probus Gardens. The soil has been treated to allow different colours to be grown in the same area (Clethra Matthews)

grown plants can be treated with an acidifying agent such as Sequestrene to encourage the blue colour. The authors feel that blues are the more attractive, but it really is a question of personal taste.

There are scores of hydrangeas to choose from. One of the best for Cornwall is the blue and white lacecap 'Sea Foam'. It is excellent by the coast but not as hardy Up Country as most other types. Hydrangeas in great abundance can be seen at Trebah, where they thrive in the damp soil of the garden's lower reaches. These were originally planted to produce cut flowers for the London markets.

Annual pruning involves the removal of three-or-four-year-old branches to their base during winter. Any weak shoots should also be removed. This keeps the plant vigorous and prevents overcrowding. In dryer soils, mulch to preserve moisture.

Fuchsia

Fuchsia splendens is one of the original species from which numerous hybrids have been bred. Although they lack the flower power of their descendants, their elegant simplicity is always admired

In Cornwall we so often take for granted our many thriving fuschia hedges. Visitors from colder climes who lovingly overwinter their fuchsias in greenhouses gaze in awe at these bountiful wonders of dripping blossom. Along with hydrangeas, fuchsias have long been valued in Duchy gardens for their enduring floral profusions. In the breeze, the flowers look like a multitude of dancing ballerinas, or, as Tim's daughter Lydia likes to think of them, angels on the wing.

This vast range of fast-growing trees and shrubs comes mainly from Central and South America, though there are others from New Zealand. Fuchsia is named after a German botanist called Professor Leonard Fuchs (apparently pronounced "Fooks"). He died more than 100 years before the honour was bestowed on him by Father Charles Plumier, a botanist and missionary. The first fuchsias arrived in Britain from the West Indies some 300 years ago, and the last century and a half has seen many hundreds of hybrids developed from the various species.

Perhaps the most widely seen here is the red-flowered *F. magellanica* 'Riccartonii' so often found on top of those soil-filled granite sandwiches we know as Cornish hedges. This tough and wind-tolerant beauty is a real Cornish classic. It can grow very large, keeps its wood during normal winters, and has a long flowering season. Regular hard pruning during February-March will keep it compact and healthy. Tougher still is *F. magellanica molinae*, which has flowers of white-flushed mauve. Other long-time favourites include *F.* 'Mrs Popple', which flowers red and violet and grows to around a metre (three feet). It is considered hardy in colder parts of the UK. *F.* 'Thalia' (see p116) is lovely in sheltered gardens, bearing clusters of long tubular-orange flowers against purple-tinged foliage. Most unlike the others is *F. procumbens*, a trailing species from New Zealand. This captivating plant has upward-facing greenish-yellow flowers baring blue pollen which was treasured by Maoris for face make-up. The berries (as with some other fuchsias) are said to be edible.

The size and hardiness of hybrids varies enormously. While a number are known to be cold hardy, it is always worth leaving some tender ones outside to test their toughness, but take some root cuttings as insurance. All fuchsias enjoy a cool, moist root run although they become more tolerant of dryer soils once established. They flower well in sun or light shade. When grown in pots they relish regular feeding.

Fuchsia magellanica 'Riccartonii' is a mainstay of the Cornish garden. As well as providing colour over a long period, it is a good wind break

Many of the flamboyant hybrid fuchsias flourish in our temperate climate, often giving us flower right through the year

29

Myrtle

The trunk of *Myrtus luma* glows more brightly than any flower when lit by the rich winter sunshine

How many gardeners can remember those moments of magic when the beauty of a special plant first struck them? One of Tim's most evocative memories is of a tree halfway between his childhood home in Avenue Road, Falmouth, and Gyllyngvase Beach. This particular treasure was growing out of the top of a low granite wall. He didn't know what it was but would stand in wonder, admiring its incredibly warm, cinnamon-coloured bark. Tim later learned that it is a *Myrtus luma*, a member of the myrtle family, and he still looks out for it some four decades hence. *M. luma*, also known as *Luma apiculata*, was introduced by William Lobb from Chile in 1843 and has been widely seen in West Country gardens ever since. It can be enjoyed in abundance at Chyverton, where there is a six metre (20 feet) tall hedge.

M. luma will eventually make a single or multi-trunked small tree. Its bark is very showy, even when fairly young, and is at its most wonderful when illuminated by the soft light of evening or winter. The leaves are small and dark green. Contrasting white flowers cover the branch tips during summer and autumn. Sweet, edible red and black fruits then follow. *M. luma* will often self-seed, sometimes prolifically. It is hardy in Cornwall in all but the worst winters when it can be cut back but will usually regenerate from the trunk. *M. luma* is sometimes seen growing Up Country and should be tried more often in sheltered spots such as in light woodland or even against a warm wall.

M. luma is more of a tree than the shrubby common myrtle, *M. communis*. This comes from Europe and Asia and has been cultivated in Britain since the

M. luma 'Penwith' in flower. This was a self-sown seedling discovered in Penlee Memorial Park, Penzance, in 1972 by the gardener Ernie Cock. Its attractive cream variegation becomes strongly tinted with pink in winter

16th century. It is has long been used in the wedding bouquets of West Country brides. Traditionally, a sprig from the bouquet is taken for a cutting. The next generation of brides then uses the resulting plant, and so on down the years. A small-leafed form *M. communis tarentina* is very wind resistant and good for gardens by the sea.

Of other myrtles which have become part of the Cornish scene, *M. lechleriana* is similar to *M. luma,* but is usually furnished with branches to the ground. The new growth in April gives the whole plant a striking golden-brown colour. It then produces a profusion of sweetly-scented flowers and is known to seed like *M. luma,* though is not as hardy. There are some fine specimens at Trewithen.

M. luma in full bloom. The display can last for weeks, then sporadically into winter. Here some of the lower branches could be removed to reveal more of the pleasing bark

Hebe

The durable *Hebe* 'Blue Gem' is virtually ever-flowering on clifftops and in Cornish coastal gardens

Scholars of mythology will know that Hebe, goddess of youth, brought nectar and ambrosia to the gods to keep them young. This is a fitting image for a robust and pretty shrub, especially those varieties which flower over many months and bring such a fabulous vibrancy to our garden scene.

There are more than 100 species of this popular evergreen. Most come from New Zealand, where, as in Britain, hebe used to be known as veronica. We have chosen to feature *Hebe* 'Blue Gem', perhaps not the most ornamental of the group, but a very durable plant and a classic constituent of Cornish coastal gardens. It is in fact a hybrid raised in Salisbury, Wiltshire, circa 1868. In gardens it is a dome-shaped, gradually-spreading plant, reaching a height of around a metre (three feet) or more. It can easily be clipped to restrict its dimensions. The violet-blue flowers are borne over many months, sometimes even during winter. 'Blue Gem' has proved extremely tolerant of our salt-laden winds and has been used extensively for hedging on the Isles of Scilly, where it is known as hedge veronica and is often seen growing out of walls. Down the years, it has self-seeded along the Cornish coast, often appearing in somewhat stunted form. Taller than 'Blue Gem' is *H. x andersonii*, which should be more widely planted again since its demise in the cold winters of the 1980s. It and 'Blue Gem' both have very effective variegated forms.

There are scores of other hebes suited to Cornwall, varying in size, colour and flowering time. Two more to look out for are *H.* 'Simon Delaux', which carries large clusters of crimson flowers in summer, and *H.* 'Great Orme', which blooms bright pink through the warmer months. All of the above should succeed in gardens which usually avoid hard frost. The dwarf, low-growing types such as *H.* 'Red Edge' are usually fairly hardy and are often used for ground cover, contrasting well with bold plants such as phormium (pp 86-87). There are a number of other hardier types also suited to colder areas Up Country. Before choosing a hebe for your garden it is well worth taking a look at a selection in a garden such as Probus, which exhibits a wide range.

Hebes like full sun and well-drained soil. Most can be pruned very hard almost back to ground level if required. Depending on variety this may be desirable every three-four years to counter any leggy growth, and is best done in early spring.

Although not particularly frost hardy, *H. x andersonii* 'Variegata' (above) is a fast-growing and wind-tolerant favourite. The flowers appear in summer, while the cream-coloured leaf margins are attractive during winter

The delicate catkin-like flowers of *H. salicifolia* rather belie its toughness (Clethra Matthews)

New Zealand Daisy Bush

Olearia x scilloniensis, smothered in the white flowers that give it its other name, New Zealand daisy bush

Salt spray carried on winds sweeping in from the ocean. Fields shrouded in mist. Cloudy skies. Frequent showers. Snow or hard frosts a rarity. Sounds familiar? Well, we're not describing Cornwall here but the Chatham Islands off the east coast of New Zealand, which have a similar climate to ours. Hardly surprising, then, that plants from this faraway botanical wonderland do so well down here. In particular, *Olearia traversii* (known as *akeake*) has become one of the great unsung heroes of Cornwall. This daisy bush has rather modest flowers and is frost tender, but is incredibly tolerant of salt winds and can be planted right by the sea, even in sand dunes. It is also a fast grower. It can reach two metres (seven feet) in two years and can eventually grow up to six metres (20 feet). It has been used as a hedge on the beach side of Queen Mary Gardens to great effect.

There are around 130 species of olearia, all native to Australasia. Many combine stout wind resistance with beauty in flower. Most are not cold hardy so are not encountered much in inland Britain. They tend to have thick, leathery leaves in dark green or grey-green, sometimes with a contrasting underside of white or silver, giving them a shimmering effect when blowing in the wind. The flowers are usually white or cream.

An attractive "local" is *O*. 'Zennorensis', a hybrid originating at Eagle's Nest, Zennor, one of the windiest gardens in Britain, when owned by that great plantsman W. Arnold-Forster. It is distinguished by its dark glossy leaves, which always look pristine, and is also excellent near the sea. *O. x scilloniensis* is another product of

Cornwall, or Scilly to be exact. This chance hybrid was found on Tresco and is one of the finest of the family, being smothered in May by white blooms, an effect not unlike a smaller-flowered Michaelmas daisy. Similar types are *O.* 'Henry Travers' (lilac), *O. semidentata* (white) and the Tasmanian daisy bush *O. phlogopappa* (blue, lavender or rose).

O. macrodonta, known as New Zealand holly due its leaf shape, is again an excellent choice for Cornwall, and is being increasingly planted Up Country. The whole plant gives up a pleasant musky odour and is covered in fragrant daisies in June. It can grow beyond three metres (ten feet) and eventually become a small tree.

Daisy bushes enjoy well-drained soils and plenty of light. They will tolerate hard pruning, preferably in early spring.

The perfect deployment of an *Olearia traversii* hedge. It takes the full onslaught of salt-laden south-westerly gales in its stride

Olearia 'Zennorensis', a native of west Cornwall. Its distinctive leaves always seem in perfect condition

Pittosporum

Pittosporum tenuifolium 'Silver Queen'. 'Pittos' provide impressive structure and leaf colour to many a Cornish garden

Yet another import which bears out the special Kiwi-Kernow relationship. The upright, immaculate-looking *Pittosporum tenuifolium* is the most popular hedging plant in New Zealand, where it is known as kohuhu. Traditionally it was used as a herbal remedy for halitosis and colds, and also provides food for a variety of birds and possums. Over the last two centuries it has firmly established itself here as an attractive hedging plant and good wind resister. It is also arguably the most popular shrub for the UK cut flower market and helps make up many a floral arrangement.

In the garden it is usually seen as a shrub but will grow into a tree given time, and specimens of 15 metres (50 feet) or more have been recorded at Tregrehan in the past. Young shoots are black, providing a fine contrast to the glossy, crinkly leaves which range in colour and grow to between three to seven centimetres in length. The flowers are dark purple, almost black. Though inconspicuously small, they carry a strong, honey-like fragrance, which is at its most powerful in the evening, and detectable from some distance.

There are many types to choose from. 'Garnettii' has white margins to the leaves which become pink tinted in winter. 'Purpureum' has pale green leaves which change to bronze-purple (tender Up Country). The smaller, silvery-green leaves of 'James Stirling' give a dainty effect. 'Warnham Gold' has young greenish leaves maturing to a golden yellow. All look good catching the winter sunshine, when the leaves appear to glow.

Generally, pittosporum does well in Cornwall and several nurseries stock a good range. It is also grown commercially and "exported" to England from some major nurseries, including the Tregothnan estate. As a hedging plant it can easily be clipped to size but does not enjoy heavily salt-laden winds. Most soils are suitable if not too wet. In chillier climates, position away from cold winds in sun or light shade, avoiding frost pockets. New varieties of *P. tenuifolium* such as 'Elizabeth' and 'Victoria' are said to be more cold tolerant. Slower-growing forms such as 'Green Elf' and 'Tiki' and the richly purple-leaved 'Tom Thumb' are ideal for containers if protected from the worst of the cold weather. Similar to *P. tenuifolium* but on a larger scale is *P. eugenioides*, seen to great effect at Lamorran. *P. tobira* is a showier, slower-growing species widely seen around the Mediterranean as hedging. The leathery, polished leaves have a good salt tolerance and the creamy white flowers give a lovely orange-blossom scent in the late summer and autumn. Definitely a shrub which should be more widely planted in Cornwall.

P. t. 'Warnham Gold'. Position coloured-leaved types so that they catch the rich winter sunlight

The distinctive leaves of *P. t.* 'Garnettii'. Most of the tenuifolium types are popular in floristry for their attractive and long-lasting cut foliage

Eucalyptus

Many eucalyptus (gum trees) exhibit this open-branched style, which shows off the attractive bark. When the wind blows, the entire tree will sway, while the leaves shimmer in just a breath of breeze, playing the light beautifully

There are more than 500 species of these captivating evergreens from Australia. In their native land they are known as gums because of the sticky stuff which exudes from the bark of some species. Their fast growth rate makes them suitable for timber and fuel and for quick shelter and screening. They also provide koala fodder, essential oils and cut foliage for florists. The first seeds were brought back from Down Under to Kew in the 1770s and since then the history of eucalyptus in the UK has been one of trial and error. Many species grown here have previously been considered tender, but in recent years careful sourcing of seed from trees growing at high altitudes has resulted in plants more tolerant of UK winters. At least 20 types are now proving reliably hardy.

Among the gums there is a wide range of leaf shape and colour, including greens, blues, greys, silvers and powdery whites. Even the same species exhibit young and adult leaves which can be quite different. Eucalyptus is related to the bottlebrush and its flowers are similar in shape, appearing as creams, yellows or reds. Unfortunately the spectacular yellows and reds are less hardy and only occasionally succeed in Cornwall. An exception is the brilliant red *Eucalyptus ficifolia*, which thrives on Tresco and generally does well in sheltered corners of the far south-west. It is superb in bloom and makes good cut flower and foliage. Grown from seed, it should flower in three-five years. It is also suitable as a pot plant provided it has a large container and is protected from frost. It can be cut back when it gets too big. Two others that are well proven in Cornwall

The gorgeous *Eucalyptus ficifolia*, one of the toughest red-flowered gums. It deserves to be more widely planted in warmer spots, then replanted if periodically killed by frost. It is *that* wonderful

The flowers of the hardy gums tend to be less conspicuous but no less delightful, and are worth looking out for in late summer

are *E. pauciflora* (snow gum) from Victoria, and *E. niphophila* (alpine snow gum) from New South Wales.

Most gums are fairly tolerant of wind but should be protected from the full force of salt-laden or very cold blasts. Because these trees are fast growing, it is recommended they be planted at less than a metre (three feet) high to ensure the top doesn't outgrow the roots, or they may blow over. To aid this, cut back plants to 25-45 cms (10-18 ins) from the ground in the spring a year after planting to encourage a good root/top balance. One new shoot can later be selected as the new leader and the others removed, or leave several to take on a multi-trunked effect.

Mimosa or Silver Wattle

Covered in blossom, the mimosa (*Acacia dealbata*) provides a glorious show early in the year (Roy Cheek)

With the acacia family numbering more than 1,000 members, and about 20 types seen in Cornwall, we were again rather spoilt for choice. We opted for the fast-growing mimosa, which is widely seen here. It has a fascinating history in its native Australia, where it is known as silver wattle and thrives on riverbanks and slopes. There the indigenous Koori people used the wood for axe handles and the gum to fasten the stone heads. European settlers are said to have taken the gum with milk for diarrhoea and dysentery. They soon recognised the beauty and versatility of this feathery-leaved tree and began sending seed back to their homelands. Mimosa, properly known as *Acacia dealbata*, also yields good quality timber. This varies in colour from light brown to pink and has had a variety of uses from coffins, to furniture, to clothes pegs. We've even heard of it being used in aircraft manufacture.

Mimosa is also highly valued for its yellow blooms, which appear in January and February and exude an intoxicating scent on calm, sunny days. Cut flowers sold in the UK are mostly imported from the French Riviera. In Cornwall many specimens have been badly damaged during sporadic hard winters but have usually re-grown from the trunk. Owners of smaller gardens should note that a mimosa can grow to eight metres (26 feet) or more so it needs careful positioning. It is best grown with some shelter so the blooms are protected. A form known as *A. dealbata subalpina* is from a higher altitude and therefore should be hardier.

Another acacia now widely seen in Cornwall is Ovens wattle (*Acacia pravissima*). Its small, triangular-shaped, blue-green leaves and pendulous branches make it quite different in appearance. It is a spectacular sight when in full flower in April. A number have been cleverly grouped together at Trebah where they "weep" enchantingly over a path. Ovens wattle is more cold hardy than the silver type so it is more suitable for a sheltered spot in Up Country gardens. This relatively new addition to the Cornish scene is slower growing and its smaller size makes it a better bet for more modest plots.

Acacias prefer a well-drained acid or neutral soil. They should be kept well watered when young, although once established they are fairly drought resistant for two or three years. They enjoysunbut will tolerate light shade and are easily grown from seed.

Cascades of flower grace the Ovens wattle (*Acacia pravissima*) in spring

Prickly Moses (*Acacia verticillata*), distinguished by its dark green needle-like leaves. All three types pictured have quite different foliage, demonstrating the diversity of the group (Mike Nelhams)

The Montereys

The Monterey cypress (*Cupressus macrocarpa*, above) and Monterey pine have long been valued for their salt wind tolerance, and have been extensively planted to help provide shelter for more delicate exotics

Whoever said that Cornwall is the California of England may well have had in mind a vision of these noble trees standing sentinel on some lonely, wind-blasted headland above a rocky bay. The Monterey pine (*Pinus radiata*) and Monterey cypress (*Cupressus macrocarpa*) are both native to the cliffs of the scenic American peninsula which gives them their common names. Since they were first introduced here in the 19th century, these fast-growing, salt-tolerant giants have become our trademark conifers, belying a perception of the Cornish shore as a bleak and treeless place.

Reaching heights of around 24 metres (80 feet), the pine has a stout trunk with deeply-fissured bark and a dense head of greenery. When establishing Tresco Abbey in the 1830s, Augustus Smith chose Monterey pines to protect his expanding garden, helping to transform this previously barren island into a paradise of plants. Many other Cornish gardens took a leaf out of his book and did the same. The life expectancy of these fast-growing trees is around 100 years, but sadly new planting was less frequent after Victorian times, resulting in notable gaps appearing on the landscape in the later part of the 20th century. More recently gardens such as Glendurgan have put great emphasis on replanting their shelter belts while Cornwall County Council has run a programme to promote the planting of new Monterey pines.

Around the county, splendid mature specimens of Monterey pines and cypresses can still be admired singly or in groups. Each type has its own characteristic silhouette. The flat-topped cypress is dense and pyramidal when young, developing an open Lebanon cedar-like layered branch system as it matures. It has been known to grow up to 36 metres (120 feet) in Cornwall. There are several golden forms which are considered slightly tougher. When young, both types bear an abundance of branches from the ground. As they mature the lower branches are shed. They are somewhat tender in infancy, neither relishing the dryer atmosphere or more extreme temperatures encountered around the rest of Britain. Because of this, the far south-west has become their stronghold. As a general rule, all trees chosen for exposed positions should be planted as small as possible, preferably less than 30 cms (12 ins) in height, in order to maximise future root stability. It is folly to plant bigger specimens as they will be prone to falling over during their early years. For the same reason, feeding them to encourage faster growth should be avoided.

The rugged outline of mature Monterey pines (*Pinus radiata*) is a familiar sight around the Cornish coast. In the foreground, a large expanse of giant rhubarb (pp 58-59)

A 10-year-old golden Monterey cypress (*C. m.* 'Goldcrest'). The *Olearia traversii* (p 34) behind it has nursed the young cypress off to a good start, and will break low-level draughts when the tree gets bigger

Australian Bottlebrush

Callistemon citrinus 'Splendens' is one of many bottlebrushes which can be grown in Cornwall. Although less hardy than some, it is the most beautiful in flower and thrives by the seaside

It is properly called callistemon, but no evergreen shrub is more aptly described by its common name than this lovely, long-standing favourite, which seems just as much at home here as it does in Australia. Most of the examples we see in Cornwall assault the retina with striking hues of red, but Down Under you will find an array of colours including white, green, mauve and purple. The bottlebrush bloom is unusual in that unlike most flowering plants, the petals are less showy than the stamens, which en masse produce the trademark "brush."

European plant collectors first came back with bottlebrushes from the east coast of Australia in the late 1700s. Among these species was *C. citrinus*, described in the 1889, study *The Useful Native Plants of Australia* by JH Maiden as having hard and heavy wood suitable for ship-building and implements such as mallets. Today of the several species grown in Britain, *C. citrinus* 'Splendens' is the showiest and can exceed two metres (seven feet) in height and spread. When it flowers in early summer, each branch carries a mass of brilliant scarlet stamens tipped with yellow pollen, followed by attractive, dusky pink young leaves. To add to its exoticism, the leaves exude a lemon-like scent when bruised, hence the name 'citrinus'.

Generally, bottlebrushes thrive in Cornwall and the warmer parts of the south. We know of fine examples at Trewithen and Lamorran, and David has an unpruned beauty in his garden which he reckons must be 50 years old. In Australia they are often found along the edges of swamps and watercourses. Over here, they favour sunny spots

A yellow-flowered form of *C. salignus*. Red is the usual colour in bottlebrushes but a range of other colours is available

and will tolerate some coastal exposure, but don't like cold north-easterly or easterly winds. Position in well-drained, fertile soil, preferably neutral or acid. Up Country they make ideal container plants for outdoors in all but the coldest months and are very well suited to frost-free conservatories where they can sometimes flower two or three times a year.

Other bottlebrushes to look out for include *C. rigidus*, which has good salt-wind resistance, making it suitable for seaside gardens. It produces smaller, dark-red brushes. Hard clusters of old seed capsules provide an interesting additional feature and last for several years.

C. salignus is a cold-hardier type ideal for more northerly parts and has a range of colours. *C. sieberi* is slower growing and very cold hardy but its creamy yellow flowers are not as showy.

The semi-open flowers of *C. citrinus* 'Splendens'. The large bud at the top will soon unfurl into the attractive young leaves

Protea

The king protea (*Protea cynaroides*) has one of the most amazing flowers seen in Cornwall. This showy drama queen produces only a few each year, with bud formation to full bloom taking several months

Aesthetic appeal is a highly subjective business but there are those who would suggest that the huge and stunning flower of the king protea (*Protea cynaroides)* is unsurpassed in its comeliness. The wonderful thing about this sovereign of the exotic garden is that it defies the unwritten law which says that the more spectacular the flower of a given group, the more tender or difficult it is to grow. Of the 114 or so members of the protea family, the king is perhaps the showiest and one of the easiest to cultivate. Though they were introduced to the Royal Botanic Gardens, Kew, from their native South Africa as far back as 1775, for many years the only place to see proteas out of doors in Britain was Tresco Abbey Garden. In the last decade or so they have started to be grown on mainland Cornwall, notably at Queen Mary Gardens and at Lamorran.

The king protea is widely distributed in the south-western and southern parts of South Africa, where it is also known as king sugarbush and is the national flower. It will grow to over two metres (seven feet), producing succulent, spoon-shaped, and somewhat leathery leaves in a rich mid-green. A chalice of brightly-coloured bracts of pale pink to crimson surround the white, tightly-clustered tubular flowers. These usually appear in summer-autumn and are attractive to birds and bees. One of the natural wonders of South Africa is seeing the head of a long-tailed sugarbird disappear down into the centre to extract the nectar.

The increasing popularity of proteas in Cornwall is largely to do with their greater availability from nurseries. Though they are said to be tricky to grow, their basic requirements are not too hard to satisfy.

Choose a sunny corner of the garden with a very well-drained acid soil. Avoid standard fertilisers that contain phosphates as these will kill members of the protea family. Good air circulation around the plant is important, particularly in winter, so confine fleece protection to cold snaps. The king will take several degrees of frost. If cut down in a hard winter, mature plants will often regrow from the base. In colder parts of the UK, grow in a large pot following the same principles.

Another protea to look out for is *P. eximia*, recommended by Mark Brent of Lamorran as a tough, lime-tolerant and fast-growing type.

Protea pioneering is long established on the Isles of Scilly but on the mainland it is still in its infancy. This *P. subvestita* is showing great promise. Its origins in high-altitude South Africa make it fairly hardy

Princess protea (*P. grandiceps*) is from the upper reaches of the Cape. Although slow growing, it has a long flowering season and good wind tolerance

Three California Dreamers

Perfectly at home in Cornwall, the tree anemone (*Carpenteria californica*) gives a glorious floral display during early summer

Despite the difference in sunshine levels, there are a number of plants from California which thrive in Cornwall. We've picked out three shrubby lovelies which should be more widely seen as they provide some of the most beautiful flowers we can grow. Naturally enough, all should be given a sunny position.

The first is the California tree poppy (*Romneya coulteri*), also known as dream of the desert. It is distinguished by gorgeous flowers which look like crinkly white tissue paper and grow to 15cms (six inches) across. These are produced from mid-summer and exude a delightfully-sweet scent on hot days. The tree poppy is capable of reaching three metres (ten feet) in height but is usually around half that. The leaves are grey-green and fleshy with a good resistance to salt winds. Romneya forms a spreading clump and as it grows, suckers can emerge from the root system at some distance from the mother plant. It is hardy in much of Britain once established in a warm spot. Cut out old stems as they become tatty or die back in winter.

A close relative is *Dendromecon rigida*, also known as the bush poppy, first introduced to the UK by Cornwall's own William Lobb in 1854. It forms a small shrub with a framework of stiff, upright branches and pointed blue-green leaves. The fragrant, buttercup-yellow flowers are much smaller than romneya, but are produced over a long period from spring to autumn. It enjoys heat and sunshine and not too much exposure to the wind as the brittle branches are prone to snapping off.

Our third   dreamer is *Carpenteria californica*,

The flowers of the bush poppy (*Dendromecon rigida*) are produced freely over many months if grown in a warm position

commonly known as the tree anemone. This evergreen shrub, which grows to five metres (16 feet), is now rare in its natural habitat but is proving an excellent choice for Cornwall as its narrow, leathery leaves have good wind tolerance. In June and July it bares copious clusters of white, Japanese anemone-like flowers. It is best grown against a wall Up Country, where it should be fully hardy in most sheltered gardens. Little pruning is required, other than occasionally removing older wood to maintain vigour.

All three plants prefer a well-drained soil which doesn't dry out in summer, particularly in the first year after planting. Annual spring mulching would help them greatly. While all enjoy a hot spot, they should also succeed in less than perfect conditions given the maximum available light.

The Californian tree poppy (*Romneya coulteri*) is an distinctive seaside plant which blooms for weeks into the autumn

Abutilon

Abutilon megapotamicum is seldom without flower. Much used for breeding, its descendants include the yellow 'Golden Fleece' and burnt orange 'Patrick Synge'

For the romantics among us, an evergreen shrub whose name means "from the big river" almost demands inclusion for that reason alone. The waterway in question is the Rio Grande in Brazil and the plant, *Abutilon megapotamicum*, has been a British favourite for 200 years. It comes from a family of over 100 different species popular for their bell-shaped flowers, borne plentifully over long periods, creating an exotic show. Some types lose their leaves due to frost or wind, yet can still bear flowers in the middle of a Cornish winter. Often used as wall plants, abutilons flower best in full sun, though they are tolerant of light shade. Those with a lax habit such as *A. megapotamicum* enjoy sprawling through neighbouring plants. Other types have a stiff, upright habit which makes a perfect frame for annual climbers such as the firecracker vine (*Mina lobata*). The red-topped and yellow-skirted blooms of *A. megapotamicum* appear in abundance through summer and autumn and less so at other times. This established favourite is also known – confusingly – as the Japanese lantern tree, due to the shape of the flowers, not its country of origin.

Perhaps the most popular abutilons throughout Britain are *A. x suntense* and its Chilean parents *A. ochsenii* and *A. vitifolium*, all distinguised by their large vine-shaped leaves. They have more open flowers, in shades of lavender, purple and white, and are striking when in bloom during May-July. They are fairly hardy but need support to reach their full heights of four metres (13 feet) or more, making them a popular choice for growing against a sunny wall.

Abutilon x suntense 'Jermyns' has a striking presence in the early summer garden

Several other species have been hybridised – some with *A. megapotamicum* – to produce many colourful bell-shaped forms. These have been used traditionally by parks departments in summer bedding displays. They have also done well in Cornwall as permanent planting and should be seen more. They all root easily from cuttings and make good patio and conservatory plants, best grown out of doors during summer to avoid pests such as whitefly.

Tim has a special affection for abutilons because they have been championed by his mentor and friend Roy Cheek at Tim's old college, Cannington, near Bridgwater in Somerset. Roy has created several new variegated varieties which carry the name 'Cannington.'

Abutilon vitifolium 'Album' is surprisingly wind-tolerant, given its large leaves

South American Peas

The exuberant cockspur coral tree – tougher than it looks

Another spectacular plant which had a captivating effect on the boy Tim when he was a prototype plantsman is the cockspur coral tree. He well remembers being entranced by the delightfully-weird scarlet flowers peeping over the wall of a house on St Mawes seafront and we are happy to report that it is still there, having grown to two metres (seven feet). The fabulous exoticism of this member of the pea or legume family is embodied in its other names. It is botanically known as *Erythrina crista-galli*, the second part of which means cock's comb, describing the flower. Equally memorably, it is also known as crybaby tree or Christ's tears, due to the abundant nectar which drips from the flowers. In its natural habitat it thrives by rivers, lakes and marshes, and is so popular it has been granted national flower status in both Argentina and Uruguay. Traditionally its light wood is used in the making of rafts, beehives and toys. It was first introduced to Britain in the 1700s but for some reason has not been planted as widely as it should be.

The cockspur coral tree forms an extensive, woody rootstock which slowly develops a trunk in warmer areas. In late spring it sends up powerful thorny growths supporting the three-lobed leaves. For several weeks in summer, 20-30 large pea flowers appear at the end of each growth, causing them to arch under the weight.

Cockspur coral trees favour a well-drained soil in a sheltered, sunny position. In Cornwall younger specimens should be hardy enough to plant out. Up Country, choose older specimens which will be tougher, and mulch in winter to protect the rootstock. Cut back the non-woody top growth when the plant

The Argentine wild sensitive plant (*Senna corymbosa*), is seldom seen without bloom in Cornwall

has died back in winter. And be patient – this species is often late coming into growth in spring, causing concern that it might have perished. It can also be grown as a frost-tender pot plant. The smaller form 'Compacta' is well suited to this.

A second perfect "pea" for Cornwall is *Senna corymbosa*, a shrubby, scrambling beauty from Uruguay and Argentina which can exceed two metres (seven feet) in height. Also quite wonderfully known as the Argentine wild sensitive plant, it was introduced to the UK more than 200 years ago as *Cassia*. It can be left to scramble but is best trained against a sunny wall where, given a mild winter, it will produce an abundance of buttercup yellow flowers for nearly 12 months of the year. It is hardy in Cornwall and does well in sheltered gardens Up Country but may be cut back in harder winters. Established plants should re-grow from the woody branches at the base. A good tip: its leaves droop at night, making it look short of water – so don't be fooled or you may drown it!

A must for the exotic garden is the cockspur coral tree (*Erythrina crista-galli*)

Kowhai and Kaka Beak

The beautiful kaka beak (*Clianthus puniceus*) is one of many shrubs from New Zealand which thrive in Cornwall

New Zealand provides us with these two spectacular flowering members of the pea family. Both are old Cornish favourites whose numbers have dwindled over the years and really should be more widely planted.

Kowhai, also known as New Zealand laburnum, is that country's national flower and deservedly so. The great botanist Sir Joseph Banks introduced it to Britain in 1772 following his return from Captain James Cook's exploratory voyage. In its native land kowhai (the Maori word for the colour yellow) has many medicinal uses, including the treatment of itchy skin, blood poisoning and even fractures and gonorrhoea, though we can't endorse any of these. There are several types of kowhai. The most widely seen in Cornwall is *Sophora tetraptera*. The bright yellow, tubular flowers are produced in drooping clusters during spring, making a gorgeous display for several weeks. Leaves are divided into 20-40 leaflets, giving a fern-like effect. It will form a small tree but is most often an upright growing shrub. It can reach six metres (20 feet) or more, even taller in the wild, and looks wonderful in full flower against a blue sky. It is hardy in all but the very worst Cornish winters and can be grown in sheltered spots in much of the UK if given protection when young. Another variety, *Sophora* 'Sun King', is smaller growing but much hardier.

Kaka beak (kaka is Maori for parrot) is another New Zealand beauty brought back by Banks. Its botanical name is *Clianthus puniceus*, and it is also known as red kowhai and lobster's claw. This stunning plant, less hardy than the kowhai, is now extremely rare in its North Island natural habitat but

still provides one of the most exotic blooms seen outdoors in Cornwall. Its brilliant red flowers are carried in pendulous clusters, freely borne from late winter for many weeks. There are also white and pink forms but the red is by far the showiest. The leaves are similar to the kowhai but this is a shrubbier plant with a scrambling habit which will only reach three metres (ten feet) even if supported. It is enjoyed by slugs and snails so take precautions. Like kowhai, kaka beak can be pruned hard, preferably after flowering. It is often trained against a sunny wall and was a prominent feature in Penzance during the middle of the last century. There are lovely examples growing in the walled gardens at Trewithen. A new form called 'Kaka King' is said to be more cold hardy and should be worth seeking from specialist nurseries. In colder air than Cornwall's, kaka beak makes a good cool conservatory plant.

The kowhai (*Sophora tetraptera*) breaks into a profusion of bright yellow flowers during early spring

The long, sprawling growths of the kaka beak are well suited to wall training (Roy Cheek)

Tree Fern

These tree ferns (*Dicksonia antarctica*) have thrived for years in the sheltered Jungle at Heligan, where the moisture and humidity ensure luxuriant growth

Legend has it that the first of these majestic plants arrived in Cornwall as ballast in the hold of a ship returning from Australia. They were unloaded on the quayside where, so the myth continues, they were spotted by an opportunistic gardener and planted. The truth is more likely to be that Treseders, the famous nurserymen based in Truro, set up in New South Wales and sent them back as huge dried logs, sawn off with no roots. They were then thrown into the river and rehydrated. Heligan, Caerhays and Trebah were notable recipients of the early arrivals in the second half of the 19th century.

There are many types of tree fern. The hardiest and therefore the commonest in Cornwall is *Dicksonia antarctica*, from south-eastern Australia and Tasmania. Here they thrive in moist woodlands similar to their homelands. Today no great Cornish garden seems complete without its grove of these stately giants. Heligan in particular has suited them and now boasts some of the largest specimens in the British Isles, growing to six metres (20 feet) or more in the Jungle. A particularly fine avenue graces the lower garden at Penjerrick and there are some hefty specimens at nearby Carwinion. Other places to see them include the spectacular fern pit at Trewidden, on the site of an old opencast mine, and at neighbouring Trengwainton.

The trunk of a tree fern is made up of the fibrous remains of its old roots. Only the top 30-40cms (12-15 ins) of the tree is alive. This sends new roots down the trunk to the ground each year and produces a new set of fronds (fern leaves) each spring. This is fascinating to watch as, over a

A classic image of tree ferns at Trengwainton. Dicksonia is not the only type worth planting in Cornish gardens. The black (*Cyathea medullaris*) and silver (*Cyathea dealbata*) tree ferns are magnificent types, but are only suited to warmer gardens

The lower garden at Penjerrick. Tree ferns combine with stagnant ponds and narrow paths to make it even more jungly than Heligan

period of about three weeks, the fronds unfurl from the crown like a series of springs uncoiling in extreme slow motion. Tree ferns are best grown out of the hot sun and should not be allowed to dry out, particularly when newly planted, so apply water generously and often into the crown in summer.

If a log (as opposed to a pot-grown specimen) is purchased the base can be planted. But with an annual growth rate of three cms (just over an inch), and as you buy them per foot, you could be burying a lot of money. Instead, you can just stand the logs on the ground and stake them firmly. In two-three years they should be well rooted.

D. antarctica is hardy enough to be grown in most parts of the UK. It enjoys a sheltered position out of drying winds. Protect the top 60 cms (two feet) of trunk in early winter with a thick layer of insulating material such as straw. Retain this with chicken wire and remove in spring. Tree ferns look superb singularly or in groups next to water and combine beautifully with gunnera, bamboo, phormium and chusan palm to create a "jungly" feel.

Giant Rhubarb

Giant rhubarb (*Gunnera manicata*). Early spring sees the emergence of the flowers and leaves of this strange South American moisture lover

This monster of the bog is a lot of fun to have in the garden. As well as its erroneous popular name (it has nothing to do with the crop which goes with custard), it is also known light-heartedly as dinosaur food, the poor man's umbrella plant and elephants' ears. *Gunnera manicata* is the proper name for one of the world's largest herbaceous plants. It is named after one J.E. Gunnerus, a Norwegian bishop and botanist, and originates from the South American swamps stretching from Southern Brazil to Columbia. It has become equally at home in muggy Cornwall since its introduction to Britain in the 1860s as something of a Victorian freak. Every great Cornish garden has to have a giant rhubarb patch. The lower reaches of Trebah, the Jungle at Heligan, and St Just-in-Roseland Church immediately spring to mind.

Though unrelated to rhubarb, the two plants are similar in leaf shape and appearance. The difference is in sheer scale. In winter, the top of the moisture-loving giant variety dies back to the ground, leaving only a collection of huge pink hairy-looking buds. New growth starts early in Cornwall. Leaves are preceded in spring by the strange flower heads up to one metre (three feet). If not damaged by frosts, by mid-summer the plant can easily reach a staggering four metres (13 feet) in height with leaves 2.5 metres (eight feet) across, big enough to provide shelter in a downpour.

When plants become scruffy in early winter, traditionally the old leaves are sliced off. The stalks are removed, then the leaves are arranged upside down over the crown of the plant. This provides frost-protection, though gunnera is hardy enough

An imposing and rather sinister stand of giant rhubarb at Trebah, guaranteed to capture any child's imagination

to survive Cornish winters unaided. There is another reason for this practice – the decomposing leaves enrich the soil. As an added bonus, this avoids having to remove masses of large leaves from the gunnera colony, which at places like the Jungle would be impractical and very time consuming.

Giant rhubarb can be grown in a large, well-watered container. It can cope with full sun provided it doesn't dry out but also thrives in light shade. As with most plants with big leaves, it's best to avoid windy sites. However, the colony on the island at Queen Mary Gardens copes very well even though it's just a stone's throw from the beach. In colder areas young plants will need protection for several years, as they are less hardy than mature ones.

A similar species is *G. tinctoria*, which grows to about half the size of *G. manicata* and would be more suited to a smaller garden. We have even read that in its native lands of Columbia, Ecuador and Chile the leaf is eaten. Perhaps with a large dollop of the local custard!

Not surprisingly, these bizarre flower heads have yet to become part of the Cornish cut-flower industry

Banana Tree

A magnificent clump of Japanese banana (*Musa basjoo*) at Trengwainton. The tallest stems are near to flowering size, while several new ones are produced from the roots each year

For more than 100 years, the huge paddle leaves of the banana tree have cast their graceful shadows over many of the great Cornish gardens. The most popular type grown here is *Musa basjoo*, which is originally from China. Confusingly, it is commonly known as the Japanese banana, because it was widely cultivated on the Ryukyu archipelago of Japan, an island chain famous for its healthy diet and the long life-expectancy of its inhabitants, and was originally imported to the UK from there.

Though surprisingly easy to grow, in the Britain you won't reap edible fruit from these ornamental beauties. Not that this discouraged one enterprising gardener at Trebah many years ago. For extra effect, he is said to have hung a bunch of shop-bought bananas from a tree in an attempt to fool a royal visitor to the Helford River garden into believing that they grew there! While at Heligan in the mid-1990s, Tim did his bit for the magical musa by planting a grove of more than 30 individuals in the Jungle.

The stem of the banana tree is made of tightly-wrapped leaf sheaths. It can grow to three metres (ten feet) and the leaves can reach a similar length. As with all bananas, each new leaf is bigger than the last. These can easily become shredded if exposed to strong winds, though this does not harm the plant. Each stem is monocarpic (it dies after flowering), while new stems are produced from the base each year to form a clump. Don't panic if your musa appears to wilt and die during cold weather, as the leaves will be blackened by moderate frosts but regrow from the top of the stem in spring. In cold weather the trunk can be wrapped for protection but this isn't normally necessary in Cornwall. In areas prone to very hard frosts, the roots may also need protecting.

Not as hardy as the musa – but arguably more beautiful still – is the *Ensete ventricosum* or Abyssinian Banana which hails (as the name suggests) from east Africa. The ensete's stem is shorter and wider than the musa. Its leaves can grow to an amazing four metres (13 feet) long and are distinguished by a stunning red mid-rib when viewed from below. In all but the warmest Cornish gardens, ensete should be container-grown or, if planted, be containerised for winter, kept frost free, and planted again in May.

It takes about five years for a stem of the Japanese banana to flower, then a long, arching head appears from its top

The huge, sail-like leaves of the Abyssinian banana (*Ensete ventricosum*) make it arguably the most spectacular of all Cornish plants

Monkey Puzzle

The distinctive silhouette of the monkey puzzle (*Araucaria araucana*) makes it one of the easiest trees to recognise

These strange and ancient conifers, said to have graced the earth since the days of dinosaurs, were given their popular moniker in a Cornish garden. Back in 1834 a lawyer called Charles Austin first set eyes on one at Pencarrow. "That tree would puzzle a monkey," he said. And so the name stuck. The proper name *Araucaria araucana* derives from the Araucani Indians of Chile, where the tree originates. Traditionally the monkey puzzle's resin was used in the treatment of wounds, and the Indians ate the nuts. It is said that the serving of nuts as a dessert to a party of European explorers led to the early introduction of the trees into Europe in the late 1700s. The first major consignment of seed to find its way back to Britain was collected by William Lobb in the 1840s.

The monkey puzzle's dead-straight trunk and distinctive tiers of well-spaced, spidery branches create a unique silhouette, captivating many generations of children. Because of the novelty value, these stupendous trees were widely planted by Victorians, but less so since. When the authors were growing up in Falmouth in the 1970s there were many more mature trees around but most have since died of old age. Happily, there are some fine young examples growing around Cornwall in private gardens and parks. Several are making good progress at Queen Mary Gardens, planted by Tim's brother Simon. They are on a bank only yards from the beach, demonstrating their tolerance of salt winds. There are still some giant specimens to be seen in the Jungle at Heligan, where monkey puzzles occasionally self-seed from the large globular cones, and there are some vast beauties at Penjerrick.

Children are fascinated by the spidery network of prickly scales - and the idea that monkeys would be puzzled if they tried to climb these strange-looking giants

Generally, monkey puzzles are hardy in much of Britain but particularly enjoy the moister climate of Cornwall and the South West. They can grow to 25 metres (80 feet), which is off-putting for the average gardener, though they can be considered as small trees to be removed when they get too large as they look wonderful when young. They are slow to establish but after 5-10 years will grow at the rapid rate of about 60 cms (two feet) a year. They are best grown in isolation as the shape is difficult to mix with other plants.

Though *A. araucana* is considered the only frost-hardy type in Britain, several other araucarias have been grown in Cornwall from time to time including *A. heterophylla*, the Norfolk Island pine. It will succeed in sheltered spots but usually perishes in hard winters.

This monkey puzzle at Queen Mary Gardens in Falmouth is only yards from the beach. *Cupressus macrocarpa* 'Gold Crest' (left) and a hedge of *Olearia traversii* are its salt wind-tolerant companions

Bamboo

A bit of an oddity in the bamboo world, the *Chusquea culeou* from Chile has solid canes (culms). Most "boos" grown in the UK have hollow canes and originate from Asia (Mike Bell)

This family of giant grasses has spread across the globe and has hundreds of practical uses from scaffolding, to panda food, to fishing rods. In the sheltered acres of Cornwall, bamboo fever took hold in the late 19th Century when gardeners were intrigued by the first imports. Keeping up this tradition today is Mike Bell, president of the British Bamboo Society, who lives at Wadebridge and has an extensive collection. He rates England as one of the most favourable places in the world for growing temperate bamboos. Cool, humid Cornwall, therefore, holds a unique place for bamboo cultivation. So much so that enthusiasts from all over the world come here to see these plants, including scientists from the East anxious to learn about their native species growing to maturity in a different environment. Mike reminds us that west of Lanivet near Bodmin are the remains of the drying sheds and plantations of the Bamboo Cane Company, which began in the Second World War and continued for 30 years. The site remains an enchanting place for the bamboo fan.

With around 2,000 species of bamboo, choosing the right one for your garden can be bamboozling. Traditionally the most commonly seen bamboo in Cornwall was the *Pseudosasa japonica*, which flowered widely over many years and then died back but is now making a comeback. Though this is a prolific plant, the culm (cane) colour is a rather uninspiring brown-green. One of the most exotic is the *Phyllostachys nigra*, which has black culms, but it is hard to find. From the wide range available, Tim has chosen an exciting newcomer *Phyllostachys bissetii*. It has shiny, dark-green culms and leaves and, unlike many other varieties,

A giant among bamboos, this *Phyllostachys edulis* at Fox Rosehill was revitalised by regular feeding and mulching. Its canes are impressive due to their sheer size. Other types such as the *P. aureosulcata* varieties and *P. vivax* 'Aureocaulis' are highly desirable for their yellow or golden canes

A well-established *Fargesia nitida*, displaying its characteristic weeping habit. This type is also suitable for growing in large pots (Mike Bell)

appears to be very tolerant of our salt winds. The bissetii – named after American bamboo enthusiast David Bisset – is a hardy, vigorous grower and is ideal for screening and windbreaks. It quickly establishes itself and can reach heights of up to seven metres (23 feet).

Bamboos should be fed in early spring with a high nitrogen fertiliser and then mulched with an organic material such as garden compost. An old and under-performing clump of *Phyllostachys edulis* at Fox Rosehill has in recent years been mulched with leaves and grass clippings with spectacular results. The culms are now three times the height and diameter and this plant must now rate as one of the finest specimens in the land.

Ornamental Grasses

Pampas grass (*Cortaderia selloana*) is a popular seaside plant in Cornwall. The dwarf pampas above (*C. s.* 'Pumila') is a compact, free-flowering form well suited to the smaller garden

In recent years ornamental grasses have become very fashionable. The style known as prairie planting, where grasses are mixed with hardy perennials such as echinacea, usually on a grand scale, has been imported from Germany though is less widespread in Cornwall than some other parts of Britain. Of the decorative grasses particularly suited to Cornwall, here are Tim's selections —

Pampas grass (*Cortaderia selloana*) is an established fixture and has proven wind resistance. Its dense fountain of leaves produce large, erect, feather-like heads en masse from late summer, growing to three metres (ten feet) or more, often lasting into winter. Pampas is hardy in most of the UK and tolerant of all kinds of soil, proving useful on banks and seafront slopes that are otherwise difficult to plant.

Related to pampas is *Cortaderia richardii*, a gem from New Zealand where it is popularly known as toetoe (the Maori word for grass). Flowering from mid-summer, its elegant, arching plumes on long flexible stalks make an enchanting sight when dancing in the breeze. A number can be seen in gardens along the Penzance by-pass. Here is a plant which should definitely be more widely seen in Cornwall. Its hardiness is uncertain but it is well worth trying Up Country.

Hunangamoho (*Chionochloa conspicua*) is a smaller grass from New Zealand, and provides a more dainty effect than toetoe. It looks good in groups, and grows well at Trengwainton where it seems happy in the sun or semi-shade. It is not considered hardy in colder areas of Britain.

New Zealand's hunangamoho (*Chionochloa conspicua*) produces numerous airy flower heads in summer and seems perfectly at home in Cornwall

Halfway between a grass and a bamboo in appearance is the giant reed (*Arundo donax*). This comes from southern Europe and can still be seen growing wild there. It has broad, arching leaves on thick upright stems, reaching a height of four metres (13 feet) within one season in Cornwall. It can be cut to the ground in spring and will send up strong new shoots. Tim has a special interest here as he introduced the lovely form 'Macrophylla' to Falmouth in the early 1980s. Another beautiful form 'Variegata' (also known as 'Versicolor') has creamy white stripes, but is not hardy Up Country. Giant reed looks effective in a jungle or arid scene. It also provides the garden with an attractive rattling sound. As the Arabs say, "It whispers in the wind and is silent in the storm."

The toetoe (*Cortaderia richardii*) is more compact than its cousin pampas, and its graceful flower heads open earlier in summer

Restio

This well-established restio makes a fine informal feature on a meandering path at Trelissick

It's safe to say that of all the plants in these pages, the rush-like restio family is the newest to the Cornish garden scene. The reason for this is that although they like our climate, they were until recently very difficult to raise from seed. Restios come mainly from South Africa where they are also known as Cape grasses and where the leaves of some types are traditionally used in thatching. The delicate appearance of other species makes them much sought-after by flower arrangers in modern-day Britain. Like many plants from hot, dry climates, they are known to germinate freely following bush-fires, a natural mechanism to help populations succeed. But try as they might with various heat treatments, scientists were unable to duplicate the natural process, so the wider world was denied this decorative range of plants. That was until researchers at South Africa's Kirstenbosch National Botanical Garden discovered that it was smoke, rather than heat, that broke the seeds' dormancy. They then developed an absorbent paper impregnated with smoke. When dormant seeds need "smoking", you place the paper on the surface of the compost, sprinkle with water, and essence of smoke is then washed down onto the seed. The method is now widely available, and has resulted in excellent germination.

Trevena Cross Nurseries near Helston is Britain's leading grower of restios. The proprietor Graham Jeffrey has been testing more than 30 types for hardiness and beauty and the nursery's catalogue provides extensive details of types to choose from. The freely-produced flower bracts and long-lasting seed heads come in a variety of yellows, golds and browns, providing a striking contrast to the foliage.

The tall, wispy young shoots of *Rhodocoma gigantea* will develop into elegant, arching plumes of up to 3 metres (ten feet) (Trevena Cross Nurseries)

Elegia cuspidata is a fast-growing restio highly regarded as an architectural garden plant. The golden brown flowers of spring are followed in autumn by dark brown seed heads (Trevena Cross Nurseries)

Restios are clump forming, producing new shoots from below ground similar to edible asparagus. The attractive, evergreen fronds of many provide a wispy, graceful display. Height varies between types from 30 cm (one foot) to three metres (ten feet). Most are fast growing, producing strong clumps in the first season after planting, though they may take two-three years to reach their full height. The tops may be killed by hard frosts but new shoots should appear during the next season provided the roots aren't badly frosted.

Smaller types such as *Thamnochortus lucens* are suitable as pot plants but don't let them dry out, and protect from anything more than light frosts. Restios prefer a well-drained, acid soil but enjoy plenty of water during the growing season, particularly in their first year. They are tolerant of drought once established. A bark mulch retains moisture for the roots in summer and provides some frost protection in winter. In colder areas some of the hardier types can succeed in sheltered spots, though because restios are such relative newcomers, it is difficult to be exact.

Agapanthus

Agapanthus raised from seed will produce plants of variable quality, whereas specially selected varieties give more reliable results. 'Rosewarne' is a fine blue type raised in Cornwall in recent years. The Headbourne hybrids are tougher and a good choice for Up Country, as is 'Jack's Blue', a new large hardy type from New Zealand

Cornwall has had a long love affair with this summer jewel, which takes its name from the Greek agape (love) and anthos (flower), supposedly because it looks rather anatomical. But not even the most partisan of gardeners could claim that a plant with the popular epithet blue African lily is a native of these shores. These spectacular spheres of tubular flowers with narrow but sturdy stems and strappy leaves originate from South Africa, where they thrive on the coast and up into the grasslands and mountains. European settlers were first attracted to the Cape by its potential for growing and in 1652 the Dutch East India Company established a garden to stock its fleet with vegetables. Soon agapanthus and other plants were being shipped back to Europe. It was regarded as a tender plant until the 1950s and 1960s when seed was gathered from higher altitudes and breeding programmes in the UK led to a race of cold-hardier varieties. On the Scillies, agapanthus used to be grown as a cut-flower crop. Now one of the wonders of Tresco is the profusion of brilliant blue heads on the sun-bleached dunes, where they have naturalised and self-seeded over many years, and are still cropped as cut flowers.

These members of the lily family prefer a warm, sunny position in a well-drained soil. Most types are hardy in Cornish gardens, whereas in cooler climes some varieties will need the protection of a thick winter mulch. They also make superb container plants which can be kept free of hard frosts in a shed or garage. To form a dense clump, use a 30cm (12 ins) pot or wider. They can be left for years without being potted on and flower production is often increased when the plants

Lydia and Genevieve are dwarfed by this magnificent clump. This was a poor year with only 103 flower heads. Its best effort was more than 130!

become pot-bound. It is worth buying named varieties which have been propagated by division. Of the several kinds of agapanthus available, the deciduous varieties tend to be hardier than evergreen types. The flower stems of nearly all lean towards the sun and range in colour from deep blue through to white. They vary greatly in height, too. The tallest will grow to two metres (seven feet) and can have heads as big as footballs, while dwarf types are around 45 cms (18 ins). When established, agapanthus are impressive en masse. They are easy to grow from seed.

A white form combines beautifully with a Japanese banana (pp 60-61)

Ginger Lily

This lovely ginger lily (*Hedychium coccineum* 'Tara') is a relative newcomer to Cornwall and deserves to be planted more often

One man's favourite flower is another's weed, as they say, and the ginger lily (properly known as hedychium) is a plant which is not universally welcomed. These distinctive perennials are native to the Himalayas and are related to the spice ginger. They are similar in style to canna lilies, and like them became very popular with British gardeners of the Victorian era due to their bold foliage and exotic flowers. Trebah alone is said to have more than 20 kinds, but alas their names have been lost in the mists. The best-known type *Hedychium gardnerianum* (also known as Kahili ginger) is today considered an invasive pest in the tropical forests of Hawaii and parts of New Zealand where it has out-spread its welcome, even though it is an undoubted beauty. It was first introduced to Britain in 1819 but strangely is not widely grown in Cornwall, where it is hardy in warmer gardens. It is distinguished by broad spikes of clear yellow and red flowers which carry an attractive fragrance. One particular gem to look out for is 'Great Dixter', a hybrid of *H. gardnerianum* grown by that famous exotic planting enthusiast Christopher Lloyd and named after his garden. It has wonderfully scented lemon-yellow flowers and will grow to 1.2 metres (four feet).

H. coccineum 'Tara' was introduced from eastern Nepal as recently as 1966. It produces spikes of apricot-orange flowers for several weeks but has less fragrance than *H. gardnerianum,* though it is hardier and is recommended for southern Britain if given a winter mulch. This is a good, reliable flowerer which should prove a first-class choice for Cornwall. Although a little less showy, *Cautleya spicata* 'Robusta' is the earliest of the gingers to flower and flourishes at Lanhydrock and Trengwainton.

Of the recent hybrids produced in the United States, the most promising looks to be *H.* 'Pink V', sometimes called *H.* 'Tropical Passion'. It has fragrant cream flowers with a pink splash and will reach 1.5 metres (five feet).

Generally, ginger lilies thrive in full sun with plenty of moisture at the root in summer. In colder areas the less hardy and later flowering types can be grown successfully in large pots, kept dry and frost free in winter and stood out for the summer. Their fleshy roots (known as rhizomes) should be allowed to show above the soil surface. Be patient – established clumps will flower more freely.

An established clump of hedychium provides a sumptuous late-summer show (Mike Nelhams)

The Kahili ginger (*H. gardnerianum*) thrives in a warm position, especially if fed and watered well during summer (Roy Cheek)

Canna

Canna 'Panache' is much less blowzy than most varieties. It is one of the earliest to flower and continues for months. Its compact habit makes it ideal for patio and conservatory pots

Their big bold paddle leaves and dazzling flowers mean that cannas are definitely not for the faint-hearted. As a result, these perennial drama queens have seen their fortunes ebb and flow but are currently back in vogue. They were first introduced to Europe from South America in the late 19th century and quickly established themselves as favourites in France in particular, where many flamboyant hybrids were produced to satisfy a Gallic love of the exotic. Their fortunes dipped after the First World War but in recent years they have regained popularity.

Cannas take their name from the Greek kana, which means reed-like. They are sometimes referred to as canna lilies because of their large, upright flowers but are not related to the lily. Another popular name, Indian shot plant, was inspired by their hard, round black seeds.

Cannas grow up to 2.5 metres (eight feet) and look their best as large clumps. There are still many hybrids to choose from and recent breeding, especially in the USA, has produced yet more. The large, upright leaves vary from green to bronze with some striped with yellows, oranges and reds. The flowers are not unlike that of the gladiolus, in shades of oranges, yellows, pinks and reds, blooming in summer and autumn.

The fleshy rootstocks of many types are hardy in Cornwall, though their tops will usually die back in winter. New shoots are then produced in late spring/early summer which can be prone to slug and snail damage. In colder areas the roots can be mulched for frost protection, or potted up and kept

Cannas are at their most impressive in bold groups

Broad, lush leaves and distinguished flowers make *C. iridiflora* a must for the exotic garden

just moist and frost free. If grown in pots they can be over-wintered in the conservatory, garage or shed.

Among a choice selection of these dramatic beauties is *C.* 'Wyoming', a long-established variety with bronze leaves and orange flowers. *C. iridiflora* has green leaves and nodding, bright pink trumpet flowers. The shorter growing *C.* 'Panache' is an excellent modern form, its orchid-like flowers of pale yellow flushed pink appear over a long season. Perhaps the most spectacular of all is *C.* 'Durban', which has bronze leaves with pink veins, an amazing sight when back-lit by the sun. One of the original species *C. indica*, which produces smaller orange flowers, also thrives around Cornwall.

Cannas enjoy a hot sunny position, but plenty of water will encourage strong growth during summer. Lift, divide and replant every three-five years to keep vigorous.

Montbretia

Montbretia (*Crocosmia x crocosmiiflora*) provides a rich contrast to a purple-leaved phormium (pp 86-87)

One of the great sights of high summer is burst after burst of day-glo orange springing out from our high granite hedges. This is the montbretia, a plant so widespread, it is hard to believe that it is an exotic from South Africa which has decorated our landscape for a little over 100 years. Cornwall is of course noted for its wild flowers. This is one that can be classed as an escapee from some of our well-known country estates to the highways and byways and domestic gardens, where it has become a superb space filler.

The montbretia is in fact a hybrid between two species of crocosmia, part of the iris family. It was raised in France during the 1880s and soon introduced to England, where it proved to be hardy in much of the country. In Cornwall it has seeded itself around, enjoying the warmer, moister climate, and growing and flowering prolifically in sun or semi-shade. It is a deciduous plant which produces sheaths of fresh green grass-like leaves in the early spring, attractive in their own right and a pleasant contrast to our wild plants. The flowers appear in July and August and are most commonly deep orange, flushed with yellow, on stems 45 to 60 cms (up to two feet) high.

Many other crocosmia crosses were made in the late 19th century, producing a range of colours from pale yellow to deep red. Flower sizes vary, with some up to 10 cms (four ins) across – much larger than montbretia. Some were frost tender and died out after the First World War. In more recent years The National Trust, in particular its gardens adviser Graham Stuart Thomas, found, named and preserved a number of old varieties, among them

Dusky brown leaves or yellow flowers are not widely encountered in crocosmia, but these two elements combine beautifully in *C. x c* 'Solfatare'. It is not reliably hardy Up Country

The rescuing of old types and the breeding of new ones means there are many crocosmia varieties to choose from

C. 'Carmin Brilliant' at Trelissick. They were assembled into a collection at Lanhydrock, where they now thrive. Trengwainton also has a good range.

With the onset of milder winters and, over recent years, the breeding of new, hardier types, crocosmias are popular again in Britain and there are now a good number to choose from. Most do well in seaside gardens, apart from some of the taller types, which can be blown over in their prime. The long spiky leaves of the bigger varieties add an interesting foliage effect to the jungle garden, while the seed heads of most types often remain attractive well into the autumn.

Crocosmias quickly form dense, weed-proof clumps and it is advisable to divide them every five years, in spring. Remove leaf debris during winter before new shoots emerge. They enjoy all soils apart from wet or heavy clay, though they thrive on some moisture.

Belladonna & Crinum Lilies

An established clump of crinum lilies (*Crinum x powellii*) flowering freely in late summer

The fragrant trumpets of these two attractive bulbs from South Africa lend an air of sophistication to the summer scene. The first, *Amaryllis belladonna*, has quite a name to live up to. Amaryllis was a lovely shepherdess of ancient myth. Bella donna is Italian for beautiful lady. These striking plants are commonly known as belladonna lilies but some Cornish gardeners prefer the cheekier name naked ladies. This comes from the fact that when the purple flower stems appear in August-September, the leaves of spring and early summer have already died off, leaving the ground bare. The stems produce an exotic head of warm pink flowers which deepen to crimson with age. The show lasts for several weeks and a strong established clump can be packed with stems. They flower better in the adversity of poor dry soils, so do not feed, and they like a hot spot, such as the base of a sunny wall. The strap-like leaves will require protection in colder areas but cope comfortably with most Cornish winters. They do well at Glendurgan and Trengwainton and are even grown as a commercial cut flower on the Isles of Scilly. Gardeners have been known to protect the naked ladies' modesty by planting them with that other Cape favourite, agapanthus (pp 70-71), whose evergreen leaves provide an attractive undergarment.

Their bigger cousin is the crinum lily (*Crinum x powellii*). This popular hybrid is more free-flowering than either of its parents, *C. bulbispermum* and *C. moorei*, which are sometimes seen in Cornish gardens. Crinums are remarkable for the sheer scale of their deep-rooted bulbs, which often reach the size of footballs and have long, slender necks showing above the ground. New leaves, longer and

Thriving in adversity, the belladonna lily (*Amaryllis belladonna*) produces more flower stems when growing in poorer soil

wider than those of the belladonna lily, grow in spring. In August *C. x powellii* produces a number of 1.2 metres (four feet) stems, each supporting a cluster of sweetly-scented trumpet flowers opening successively over several weeks. Rose pink is the norm, though deep pink or white forms are also available. Crinum lilies are hardy enough to thrive in much of southern England. They enjoy a richer, moister soil than belladonnas, but too much feed will result in excess leaf and fewer flowers. Both belladonna and crinum lilies enjoy a well-drained soil. They need little attention and clumps are best left undisturbed for years.

A wonderful late summer show – the gorgeous trumpets of the belladonna lily

Cornish Palm

The Cornish palm (*Cordyline australis*) in fruit. The large heads of pale berries provide a wonderful display in early autumn

With its slender trunk and leaves like green swords, Cornwall's trademark palm is the plant many visitors like to take home with them. So it may be a surprise to find that it's neither a true palm, nor Cornish, but a member of the lily family which comes from New Zealand. *Cordyline australis,* as it is properly known, was first introduced as seed to Cornwall in the 1820s. Today, these durable lovelies are seen in just about every public park, seafront and large garden. In Falmouth they lend an exotic air to the main approach to the town and there are many in and around Penzance. On Tresco, there is a glade of huge specimens between the garden and the Great Pond.

This eye-catching stalwart has almost as many names as leaves. To the Maoris, who ate the tender tip of the trunk, it is the cabbage tree. They even sun-dried the pith and inner roots to make porridge. To many in the West Country, it remains the dracaena palm, because that's how it used to be classified botanically. Just to complicate matters, it is known as the Torbay palm by Devonians who like to claim it as their own. Naturally, we prefer the name Cornish palm for this near-hardy favourite, which flourishes in mild air and can reach ten metres (33 feet) in height. In days gone by when fisherman from France came ashore along the south coast they would ask gardeners for broken branches to sharpen their knives. And for years the waste-not-want-not Cornish have used the dead leaves as plant ties.

Cornish palms can be bought at garden centres or raised from seed. They are in their glory in late spring when they produce long slender heads

In avenues or glades, Cornish palms en masse create an exotic effect

massed with tiny cream flowers giving off a powerful fragrance. They thrive in all but heavy or waterlogged soil and are seldom damaged by cold. Further north, protect from heavy frost by tying the leaves to a point and wrapping the whole plant with fleece. A group of ten or more, spaced three-five metres (10-16 feet) apart, will develop into an attractive glade. If you prefer a desert-island feel, space several trees 60-90 cms (two-three feet) apart in a group.

C. australis and its various forms grow at a rate of about 60 cms (two feet) a year. Less common is a more exotic-looking cousin, *C. indivisa*. This sturdy, single-stemmed version can reach around six metres (20 feet) in height and is distinguished by its single trunk and wider bronze-green leaves of up to one metre (three feet).

The elegant but rare *C. australis* 'Variegata', sporting its bright, creamy leaf margins. Similar but more widely available is *C. australis* 'Torbay Dazzler', which has an additional red stripe along the centre of the leaf. The best purple-leaved types are *C. australis* 'Red Star' and 'Torbay Red' which are very popular

Chusan Palm

With its trunk fur removed, this chusan palm (*Trachycarpus fortunei*) at Fox Rosehill takes on an even more exotic air

If there is one plant which has come to symbolise the wonders of the far south-west it is the magnificent chusan, the best-known and most widely seen true palm in Britain.

The huge specimens rising out of the primordial mists at Trebah and Heligan seem to capture the very essence of "subtropical Cornwall", the evocative brand image dreamed up by some ingenious Victorian Tim Smit. The irony is, the chusan may look as though it has wafted in from a desert island, but in reality it would be a fish out of water in the tropics. Its natural habitat is the Himalayan forests of China where it can grow at elevations up to 2,500 metres (8,200 feet) in high rainfall and survive temperatures as low as minus 20 degrees C.

This single-trunk palm with fan-shaped leaves is properly known as *Trachycarpus fortunei*, after the Scottish plant hunter Robert Fortune, who first brought it back to Britain. The leaf arrangement gives it its other popular name, Chinese windmill palm. Similar in appearance is the less hardy but more wind-tolerant dwarf fan palm *(Chamaerops humilis)*, which is clump-forming and often develops several trunks with age.

In its native country, the chusan's trunk hairs – thought to have evolved as a natural fur coat for insulation – are used to make ropes and coarse garments. After one specimen was set on fire at Fox Rosehill, the gardeners removed the lower hair of the others to prevent a repeat attack, thus making the trunks look thinner and the tops bigger – more like the classic desert island palm. Just

These fine specimens help make St Just-in-Roseland the most exotic churchyard in the land

A chusan in bloom at Fox Rosehill. Flower heads appear near the top of the trunk and often produce viable seed in Cornwall

along the road from these gardens, for many years a chusan had an old coconut hanging from the top, placed there by the homeowner George Ross to kid visitors into believing that coconuts grew there!

The chusan palm is hardy in most of Britain but is most at home in Cornwall because of our long growing season and moist air. It thrives in sheltered valleys, whereas in exposed positions the leaves become damaged and tatty. Happy in light shade or full sun, it enjoys moisture at the roots although it is tolerant of a dry position. Be patient with your chusan. It will take 15 years or more to reach flowering age in the UK, when it will produce a pendulous, golden-yellow head. Chusans have been known to self-sow around Cornish gardens.

Canary Island Date Palm

Hard to believe that this is the British Isles, but date palms have thrived at Tresco Abbey Garden for more than 100 years (Mike Nelhams)

Visitors to the Canaries will be familiar with these big, handsome trees. So too will those who like to stroll along Miami Beach or the boulevards of the French Riviera, where prize specimens have a dramatic architectural impact and can change hands for the price of a sports coupe. Nearer home, three fine examples on the Ponsharden roundabout provide an exotic welcome to Falmouth, planted by Tim's brother Simon, the local parks officer, in the 1980s. *Phoenix canariensis*, to use the proper name, is one of the wonders of Tresco Abbey Garden. Date palms were first introduced there in 1894 and have now grown to 12 metres (40 feet). Our spiritual mentor Edgar Thurston reports that a large and flourishing colony of *Phoenix dactylifera*, a cousin of the *canariensis*, was discovered on the Looe dust-heaps in 1927, "doubtless arising from rejected date fruits." Many large Canary Island date palms have grown on mainland Cornwall in the past but most are known to have perished in the extremely hard winters of 1947 and 1963. The popularity of the plant is undergoing a welcome revival, especially as it is now readily available.

The Canary Island date palm is distinguished by its stocky trunk, billowing crown of feather-shaped leaves and yellow or orange fruits (said to be edible but not particularly tasty). These trees can be landscaped in pairs, groups, or, Florida-style, in rows or even avenues, and they make excellent container specimens. The date palm is not as hardy as the chusan, and some of the more exposed specimens in Cornwall are protected from early winter until late spring by having their leaves tied up. As a general rule mature plants are tougher

84

than youngsters, so protection can be decreased over the years. They love full sun and should be planted in a hot spot with well-drained soil.

There are around 3,800 species of palms. Relatively few are suitable for Cornwall. Tim's all-time favourite is the elegant *Butia capitata* or jelly palm, distinguished by its wonderfully curvaceous blue-green leaves. It is cold tolerant and should, he says, be more widely grown. In its native Brazil, the edible fruit is used to make jellies and jams, but sadly you are unlikely to see any produced under a British sky.

Similar in style to the date palm, this majestic jelly palm (*Butia capitata*) at Penzance is admired by Tim's brother Simon

These Canary Island date palms (*Phoenix canariensis*) were the first planted by Simon in 1982, starting a trend which has seen many more flourish in Falmouth and elsewhere in Cornwall

Phormium

Phormiums are available in many different styles. These vertical, sword-like leaves are typical of *P. tenax* types

This is one of the most versatile plants on the planet and is prized by modern gardeners for its architectural impact. But phormium, also known as New Zealand flax, wasn't always so popular. In his classic study *Shrubs For The Milder Counties*, the celebrated plantsman W. Arnold-Forster, of Zennor, said that the huge, sword-like leaves made such a clatter in the wind "it is likely to be a nuisance if planted close to the house", and seemed to value it only as a wind-break plant. This was in 1948 before most of the many coloured forms were introduced to the UK. The Latin name comes from phormos, meaning basket, one of the many items it is used to make in its native country. There the Maoris have also used the strappy leaves in the manufacture of shoes, shelters and mats. The fibres have been used extensively in clothing, rope-making, paper-making and fishing nets. Though the flax industry has dwindled, phormium is still cultivated for weaving and plaiting.

There are only two species, *Phormium tenax*, introduced in 1789, and *P. cookianum* (1848). Both thrive in Cornwall and have been extensively planted. To tell the difference, look at the leaves. They are upright, leathery and bronze-green in *P. tenax* and grow to about three metres (ten feet) in length. *P. cookianum* leaves grow to about half the size. They are greener and the top halves are more pendulous, giving the plant a graceful appearance. In the last 40 years much hybridising has taken place in New Zealand to produce the coloured forms which are now widely available. The numerous varieties contain combinations of green, cream, yellow, red, pink, crimson and scarlet. Hardiness varies, though all should thrive in

This phormium provides a brilliant contrast to the golden-leaved *Fuchsia* 'Genii'

Cornwall. In general, *P. tenax* and its purple forms are the toughest, while those whose leaves have a central variegation are the most tender. Phormium is very tolerant of salt winds but does well in most positions and soils, sun or light shade. It sits comfortably in the exotic landscapes of coastal towns such as Penzance, Falmouth and Looe, but perhaps does not look quite right in a Cornish hedgerow. It is effective as an isolated specimen in groups, or mixed with other exotics such as cordyline and chusan palm. Established clumps will produce flowers during summer on spikes up to five metres (16 feet) high. These are dull red, not bright or beautiful, but the whole inflorescence is striking and silhouettes well against a blue Cornish sky. Coloured forms also make excellent container plants, but will need protection from the worst of the weather Up Country.

The lax leaves of this specimen indicate that this is a *P. cookianum* type. The seed capsules of both this and *P. tenax* are an additional attraction during autumn and winter

Agave

Living sculpture: *Agave ferox* has an even stronger architectural form than *A. americana* and should be more widely planted

Just to show we are not as Kernowcentric as we might seem, here is an interesting fact from Devon: The first *Agave americana* to flower in Britain was introduced by the Rev James Yates of Salcombe in 1814. The history of this extremely versatile but very prickly succulent goes back much further. It was brought to Europe from its native eastern Mexico around 1520. Across the Atlantic, it was used to treat a variety of complaints including dysentery, fevers, jaundice and flatulence. The roots are still used to make soap, and the fibres go into rope and shoemaking. It will even furnish you with a crude needle and thread in an emergency if you cut the end of a leaf spine, leaving it attached to the underside, and pull downwards to remove a long slither of leaf surface. A little first aid may be called for if you overindulge in the plant's most famous by-product, the beer-like beverage pulque, beloved by the Aztecs. This predated by many centuries the much stronger drink tequila, which derives from the blue agave of the Sierra Madre.

The americana is the best-known agave species in the UK, where it can reach two metres (seven feet) in height. The most common form has blue-green leaves but there are several variegated-leaf types which are slower growing. It is known as the century plant because legend has it that it takes 100 years to flower. This is a fallacy as in Britain it usually takes 15-25 years to bloom, when it produces a bud like a giant asparagus-tip, up to seven metres (23 feet) high. This opens to a branched head of many yellowish-green flowers. After flowering, the whole rosette dies, but will have spawned many offshoots to perpetuate the clump. In its natural habitat, *A. americana* is used to sub-

Agave americana 'Variegata' is one of several coloured-leaved forms which can provide impact in the garden. Agaves look good in pots and respond well to being fed and watered in summer

zero temperatures at night and extreme heat in the day, so it travels well. This sun-lover dislikes excess moisture in winter, so provide very well-drained soil but feed and water well during the growing season. This also applies when growing in pots, which can be kept very dry in winter. Remove old outer leaves at their base when they become unsightly. Also, with children or pets around, it is advisable to remove the sharp tips.

Agaves become hardier as they increase in size. Glendurgan has some very fine old specimens which have periodically flowered over the years.

Seen here in flower is the lesser-known *Agave celsii*, not so vicious as many of its prickly cousins

Yucca

Taking several years to flower, *Yucca whipplei* is one of the most revered sights of the Cornish scene. Even the impatient gardener should be enticed by its poise and beauty (Mike Nelhams)

Getting on for 500 years since they first graced our soils, the beautiful yuccas still have the power to stun and amaze. This family of some 40 species originates from the arid plains of Central America and southern regions of the USA. Native Americans used the roots to make hair tonic and soap, giving the plant the common name of soapweed. They also ate the flowers, buds and young stalks. In Britain, *Yucca elephantipes* has long been popular as a foliage houseplant and is occasionally seen in sheltered Cornish gardens.

Yucca species also provide the plant world with some of its most evocative common names. *Y. aloifolia* (Spanish bayonet) and *Y. whipplei* (Our Lord's candle) spring to mind. These two are excellent choices for the Cornish garden, where they grow best in sunny spots and well-drained soil. *Y. aloifolia* has stiff, needle-pointed leaves densely arranged along the trunk, and eventually becomes multi-trunked with age. Look out for a specially attractive yellow variegated form. Fine examples of this plant can be seen at Queen Mary Gardens, and Lamorran. The stemless *Y. whipplei* forms a dense clump of narrow grey-green leaves. It is stunning in bloom, though you will have to wait five-ten years after planting to see it in its glory. The flower spike rises up to four metres (13 feet) high, bearing fragrant creamy white blooms during early summer. This is such a massive effort that, like the ensete banana, the plant usually then dies (though it sometimes makes offsets). This dramatic finale was performed by a fine specimen at Fox Rosehill in recent years.

Perhaps the hardiest and therefore best known

species throughout Britain are *Y. gloriosa* (Adam's needle) and *Y. recurvifolia* (pendulous yucca). These are similar, both developing multi-trunks to form dense bushes or trees, at which stage they should produce flower spikes annually. They are fairly tolerant of Cornwall's salt winds and can be planted in semi-shade.

The trunk-forming types are very architectural plants in the landscape, and like all yuccas look good in arid displays with puyas and agaves. They can be fed in spring and watered well in summer to encourage strong, healthy growth. The tips of the long, sharp leaves of many types are dangerous to the skin and eyes, so choose and plant with caution, especially with children around. All except *Y. wipplei* should be cut back hard if they outgrow their position. Cut branches will often root if stood firmly in the ground.

In times past, yuccas were enthusiastically bred, especially in France. As a result many different types offered by nurseries as Adam's Needle (*Y. gloriosa*) may vary. This one is distinguished by its brightly-coloured flower buds

At Queen Mary Gardens, *Y. aloifolia* 'Variegata' produces stately flowers with the added attraction of yellow-edged leaves

Beschorneria

Mexican lily (*Beschorneria yuccoides*), Cornwall's weirdest triffid, raises its rhubarb-coloured tentacles over Caitlin (John Miles)

What's in a name? Quite a bit in the case of this spectacular succulent from the semi-arid regions of Mexico. *Beschorneria* is in honour of Friedrich Wilhelm Christian Beschorner, an 18th century German amateur botanist. It is yucca-like in appearance, hence the second part of the name. Its common appellations include Mexican lily, amole and sisi. The Latin name, though a bit of a mouthful, is how it is usually known. *Beschorneria yuccoides* is easy to grow and thrives in Cornwall. The head gardener at Probus rates it his favourite architectural plant in their desert area and notes that it makes a wonderful combination with a *Wisteria sinensis* growing behind it when both are in flower.

Initially it forms a rosette of blue-green leaves about one metre (three feet) across. When it reaches flowering age (two-four years), side shoots develop and eventually a large clump forms. This is when it becomes a bizarre, even sinister-looking plant, which is not to everyone's taste but is very exotic looking and invariably provokes comment. Rhubarb-red flower stems rise from the centre of the rosettes in early spring and over a period of weeks shoot up to three metres (ten feet) long, eventually arching nearer the horizontal than the vertical. In April/May, bright green fuchsia-like flowers emerge from the showy-red bracts which occur at intervals along the upper part of the stem. The individual flowers open in succession over several weeks but the stems continue to look showy throughout the summer. Established clumps produce a cluster of flower heads all shooting in different directions, creating an amazing effect. *Beschorneria yuccoides* requires a well-drained

Like a monster from a horror film, the emerging flower stems provide a hint of the drama to follow (John Miles)

soil and sunny site out of cold winds. It is best displayed in a raised bed or planter as the additional height adds to the drama. It is very effective when the flower stems arch over a path and you can walk under them. And it associates well with other arid-looking plants such as yucca, puya and aloe. Unfortunately, the rosettes are highly attractively to molluscs and their munchings can very quickly spoil the look of the leaves. A mulch of sharp grit looks good around arid plants and can also deter pests. When established, big clumps can be split up and replanted in early spring.

This spectacular plant is generally hardy in Cornwall and inner London. In cooler areas it may require protection during cold spells and should be given a sheltered corner. It can be grown in a large container and brought inside to be kept dry for the winter.

On close inspection the flowers of the Mexican lily have an unexpected charm

93

Fascicularia

Fascicularia bicolor, dazzling star of the Cornish autumn

Its name may be a bit of a tongue-twister, but the impact of a fascicularia in bloom is instant and dramatic. The combination of scarlet-flushed leaves surrounding a pincushion of tiny turquoise flowers produces an unforgettable effect. But beware – this is also a beauty with bite. The spiky teeth which edge the leaves mean it has to be handled with care.

Fascicularia bicolor is a member of the bromeliad family, a fascinating and varied group originating in the Americas, and found from Virginia in the north to southern Argentina. Pineapples are the most famous member of the family and can today be seen growing in the pits at Heligan, where they are heated with horse manure. The near-hardy *F. bicolor*, from the coastal regions of Chile, is the most widely grown bromeliad in Cornwall.

The are two types of *F. bicolor* (also known as the sun bromeliad) which at first glance seem the same. A form with shorter, wider leaves is the most popular in Cornwall and the hardier of the two. The other has slender, more elegant foliage. Both form extensive tight-knit clumps in time. Flowering usually occurs in early autumn – so many summer visitors will miss them in their glory. There are around 30-40 flowers in a cluster, opening in succession from the centre. They are quite short-lived but the vivid red richness of the leaves remains much longer. It is this which is thought to attract the humming birds and butterflies which pollinate these lovely plants on their home ground. Fascicularias grow prolifically on Tresco and St Michael's Mount and are prominent in many public and private gardens around the Duchy. They are

With no coloured leaves to attract pollinators, *Ochagavia rosea* produces bigger, more showy flowers than its fellow bromeliad fascicularia (Mike Nelhams)

near-hardy plants which also do well in other warmer areas of Britain, if given a well-drained soil, and sunshine to promote freedom of flowering. In colder areas, protect with fleece during hard frosts. Alternatively, they can be grown as a pot plant.

Less vigorous and even better for a pot is ochagavia from the coast of Chile. Its showy, silvery pink flower heads protrude from the centre of the rosette in late summer. There is a magnificent clump measuring several metres across on Tresco.

The exquisite detail of a fascicularia. But handle with care — this beauty can bite (Mike Nelhams)

Puya

The sensational flower spike of *Puya alpestris*, complete with natural perches for pollinating birds (Mike Nelhams)

An even more spectacular – and vicious – bromeliad is the puya, a plant so striking in flower it can stop traffic. The needle-sharp, inward-pointing spines of the puya's leaf will allow you to put your hands into its heart, but it is impossible to withdraw without snagging your flesh. Birds have been known to become trapped along the spines and die in the struggle to free themselves. One theory is that the plant's roots then feed on the decaying remains.

There are 168 recorded species of puya. The two most often seen in Cornwall are *P. alpestris* and *P. chilensis*. Both come from the mountainous regions of Chile, where they are associated with medicine, knife sharpening and making fibre for fishing nets from the leaves. *P. alpestris* forms a small clump in time and the flower spike can grow as high as one metre (three feet). Its flowers are an amazing sea green and David, for one, was almost stopped in his tracks as he circled the Recreation Ground roundabout in Falmouth and first set eyes on one of the botanical world's most stunning sights. Others can be seen at Fox Rosehill, St Michael's Mount and Tresco. Its compact size means that in colder areas it will make an attractive pot plant.

P. chilensis is on a grander scale. It makes a gradually spreading clump to 1.5 metres (five feet) high, while the spectacular radio antenna-like spike can grow to four metres (13 feet), bearing flowers of greenish-yellow during spring and early summer. Clumps planted a decade or so ago at Queen Mary Gardens now present an amazing display. In its natural habitat, the main pollinator of *P. chilensis* is the Chilean starling which perches on horizontal

The emerging spike of an unidentified puya species. Many more types could be grown in Cornwall if given a favourable position

The towering spikes of the *P. chilensis* are becoming a familiar sight around Cornwall as it has been more widely planted in recent times

parts of the flower to drink the nectar. This paints the bird's forehead with bright yellow, sticky pollen. The blackbirds of Scilly have learned over the years to do the same on Tresco. *P. mirabilis* is a smaller and friendlier type, producing an arching flower stem in autumn.

As with most ground-dwelling bromeliads (some grow in trees), puyas prefer a well-drained soil and will flower best in full sun. They don't need feeding and are tolerant of winds, including our salty sou'westerlies. They are usually grown from seed. They can be divided if you are feeling brave, but remember you will slash your hands and arms in the process unless you protect them well.

Hottentot Fig

One of the wondrous sights of Cornwall – a vivid mesembryanthemum cascades over a granite wall.

The exotically-named Hottentot fig (*Carpobrotus edulis*) from South Africa is the most famous member of the mesembryanthemum family of succulents. It is distinguished by its fleshy triangular stems and attractive though sparsely-borne daisy-like flowers of pink and yellow. It is also one of the most invasive plants of the Cornish landscape and is accurately described by its more prosaic name, carpetweed. On the Lizard in particular, it has spread rampantly across cliffs and evicted large areas of native fauna such as thrift. It has been claimed that the plant gained a foothold after pieces were washed up from South Africa and took root. More likely it was brought back from the Cape on board ship after the European settlers of the 17th century became captivated by its attractiveness and useful qualities. Traditionally the water-storing leaves were made into poultices to treat burns, sores, stings and colds. It is said that the fleshy, fig-like fruits can be used to make jam, though we should stress we are no experts in plant cuisine. The Hottentot fig also has other more practical uses. In the California of a century ago it was used to stabilise soil on banks during the building of railroads. It is also used there as a fire repellent around houses.

Despite its invasiveness in the wild, Hottentot fig remains a first-rate plant for the maritime garden and in other areas if kept under control. At St Mawes it does an admirable job covering a steep bank and cascading over a big retaining wall on the seafront, softening the granite work considerably.

A considerate number of other less rampant mesembryanthemums (the name means 'midday

The flowers of 'messies' occur in a range of vibrant colours, while the wax-like surface of the leaves ensures that most types can resist salt winds

Hottentot fig (*Carpobrotus edulis*) has distinctive, narrow three-sided leaves which can colour up when it is growing in poor soils. Even then, it can go rampant and become a nuisance

flower') have long been grown in Cornish gardens. Most provide very striking displays of mauves, reds, oranges, or yellows for several weeks in spring and early summer. They can be seen extensively around the Isles of Scilly, particularly at Tresco Abbey Garden, and also at St Michael's Mount and Headland Garden at Polruan.

They enjoy being planted in soil between rocks and in crevices. Cuttings can be inserted directly into position and most will root easily if not allowed to dry out. All "messies" prefer a poor, very well drained soil. Most will tolerate only light frosts, but a number of hardier types are available from various Cornish nurseries. They need little attention, other than tidying. Up Country they can be grown in pots and kept frost free, but the relatively short flowering period of most means that there are better value-for-space plants to consider.

Pelargonium

A range of pelargoniums, including several ivy-leaved types, enjoy a well-drained position at the top of a stone wall

We could have written an entire book on pelargoniums, a range of plants which has added vivid splashes of colour to the flowerbeds, patios and window boxes of Cornwall for as long as anyone can remember. Some of these are familiar to gardeners as geraniums (see Madeiran geranium pp 102-103). Although they are in the same family, this is botanically incorrect. Pelargoniums come principally from South Africa and are not therefore particularly cold hardy. In most of Britain they are grown as house, conservatory or bedding plants, best overwintered in frost-free conditions. In the mild air of Tresco, though, they have flourished for years in the dry, sunny rockeries of the Abbey Garden and are seen all around the Scillies in private plots. They have been successfully grown in mainland Cornish coastal gardens but have been periodically killed off by harder winters and not always replanted.

Much hybridisation has occurred, particularly during Victorian times, producing thousands of varieties. These have been divided into a handful of groups. Probably the best known are the zonal types such as 'Caroline Schmidt', which have been very widely used as summer bedding in parks and private gardens. The trailing ivy-leaved types such as 'Amethyst' can be left to wander or trained against a wall, reaching two metres (seven feet) or more. The unique types are very successful on Tresco and should be tried more on mainland Cornwall as they will tolerate several degrees of frost and have a long flowering period. The less showy scented-leaved types such as 'Graveolens' (grown for its essential oil known as oil of geranium), 'Royal Oak', and 'Lady Plymouth' are

The zonal leaf markings and red flowers of this scrambling pelargonium make a pleasing contrast to the purple berberis supporting it

Scented-leaved pelargoniums provide a wide range of foliage types. They are at their most effective when planted by a path or doorway where the various aromas can be savoured

also well worth trying. Some types enjoy scrambling into other plants for support, among them 'Clorinda'. Quite different to the others is *P. papilionaceum*, an erect, large-leaved shrub growing to two metres (seven feet). Although relatively unknown, it does well in sheltered Cornish gardens, providing a fine display of lilac flowers in summer.

Pelargoniums are a classic example of tenderish plants which can be treated as fast-growing, short-term perennials. They are easily raised from cuttings which, after a hard winter, can be used to replenish your garden. They are not expensive to buy and are often seen at very affordable prices at fetes and car boot sales.

Generally, they enjoy a very well-drained soil, preferably in a raised position in sun or light shade. Many are fairly wind tolerant but should be kept out of cold blasts.

Madeiran Geranium

The Madeiran geranium (*Geranium maderense*) is an attractive foliage plant which eventually develops a glorious head of flowers

This relatively new addition has become a brilliant star of the Cornish landscape, one bound to cause great envy among the neighbours. It hails from the Atlantic island of Madeira and has established itself beautifully in Cornwall, though it remains too tender for reliable outdoor planting in colder climes.

To many, geraniums are summer bedding plants once used extensively by parks departments and popular in the home garden. These are, in fact, pelargoniums (pp 100-101), not to be confused with the real McCoy. There are around 300 species of geranium. The name derives from geranos, the Greek word for crane, because the seed pods are said to look like the bird's beak – hence the popular name cranesbill.

The Madeiran geranium (*Geranium maderense*) has long been a feature at that cradle of the new, Tresco Abbey Garden. In recent years, as winters have become slightly less cold, it has been spread to the mainland by gardeners smitten by its beauty and drama.

Like the giant echium, it takes a couple of years to reach flowering size from seed. In its second year it makes a striking foliage plant, producing a mound of up to a metre (three feet) massed with finely cut, palm-like leaves. A remarkable feature is the way that the old leaf stalks touch the ground and act as a series of stanchions, supporting the rest of the plant as it grows to full size. In its third season thousands of dark-eyed magenta flowers are borne in an enormous head up to 1.2 metres (four feet) high. It blooms over many weeks from early summer, then the whole plant usually dies. It

is an enthusiastic self-seeder and young plants can be lifted and potted up, or left where they are to mature. Thin out seedlings in the garden leaving around 50-90 cms (up to three feet) between, and delight your friends by giving them the surplus. The Madeiran geranium forms a taproot so must be transplanted when young. Also look out for *Geranium palmatum*, from the Canary Islands. It is similar but slightly smaller, with crimson-centred, purplish-pink flowers.

In Cornwall both these geraniums enjoy a sunny position, or light shade in warm gardens avoiding frosty spots. In colder areas they need a very favourable position and protecting with fleece during chilly spells. They can be nurtured in a large pot Up Country but tend not to grow as big as they will in the ground.

An established favourite on Tresco, the Madeiran geranium is seen here in perfect harmony with blue echiums (Mike Nelhams)

The striking beauty of the Madeiran geranium has gardeners smitten (Mike Nelhams)

Giant Echium

A jungle of magnificent giant echium (*Echium pininana*), with many younger plants preparing for next year's extravaganza

An oddity. A floral freak. An alien tower of flowers. A fabulous monster. A bit of a triffid. These are just some of the colourful terms used to describe a plant which, because of its propensity to self-seed, can become a weed in Cornish gardens. Giant echium is a bit like Marmite. You either love it or hate it. We adore this eccentric colossus for many reasons. It is simple and quick to grow. It produces one huge spike of small lilac flowers, sometimes surrounded by several smaller branches. It creates an eco-system of its own by attracting legions of bees and bugs. It looks wonderful en masse. When it dies after flowering it produces as many as 200,000 seeds per plant, which means if you're a fan you can be self-sufficient in echium for the rest of your days.

Giant echium (*Echium pininana*) grows wild in its native hillsides and laurel forests of the Canary Islands. Ironically, because its natural habitat is shrinking, it has become an endangered species there, while it thrives here. It is a relatively recent addition to the Cornish landscape but has taken root and spread rapidly through gardens, parks and roadsides of the county.

Giant echium is perhaps best described as 'triennial'. It usually germinates during summer with the resulting seedlings or small plants overwintering into the second year, when it forms a strong rosette of large, dark-green leaves on a very prickly trunk (handle with care). The following year the lower leaves drop away as the floral spire emerges, rapidly bursting into colour at up to four metres (13 feet). It is hardy in Cornish gardens. In colder areas, try it in a sheltered spot, protected

with fleece during winter. It can be grown in a large pot but will be less impressive than in the ground. It likes a well-drained soil, full sun and some shelter, as the shallow, fibrous roots can be dislodged by strong winds. To get a "mini-palm tree" look before a mature echium goes into flower, pull off the dying lower leaves to leave only the new, lighter green ones at the top.

Rarer, slightly smaller, and perhaps more beautiful still is the *E. pininana*'s wonderfully-named, showy cousin *E. wildpretii*, also known as tower of jewels, which produces a profusion of red flowers on a one-two metre spike covered with silver hairs. It is fairly cold hardy but much less tolerant of wet than *E. pininana* so prefers to be kept dry in winter.

The tower of jewels (*E. wildpretii*) is a little more tricky to grow due to its dislike of the wet. Not surprising, considering it flourishes naturally at the top of volcanic Mount Tiede on Tenerife (Trevena Cross Nursery)

Echium is closely related to the forget-me-not, and the family resemblance can clearly be seen here

Convolvulus

The charming buds and flowers of *Convolvulus cneorum*

The most familiar member of this family is the dreaded bindweed, that deep-rooted perennial pest which wraps itself around your favourite plants and, if left to run riot, chokes the life out of them. Not even its attractive white trumpet flowers make it anything but a rampant nuisance. It may be a surprise to some, then, that we feature this group of sun lovers, but there are a number of very desirable gardener-friendly types which should be more widely planted in Cornwall.

The most popular is *Convolvulus cneorum* (said with a silent "c"), which originates from southern Europe and was first recorded in England way back in 1640. Popularly known as bush morning glory, this compact evergreen is one of the loveliest silver-leafed shrubs. Like many Mediterranean plants it is not long lived but easily grows from cuttings. It is a first-rate foliage plant, with the bonus of a profusion of pink buds in spring, closely followed by a flush of white, yellow-eyed flowers. Blooming continues to a lesser extent through the summer. It is fairly cold tolerant but dislikes a combination of winter cold and wet which often causes its demise Up Country. It succeeds in Cornwall's damp-but-warm climate if given a well-drained, sunny and airy position away from chilly winds. The National Trust garden at Trerice features a lovely example in its drawing room border. With a spread usually less than a metre (three feet), it also makes an excellent plant for a terracotta pot in gritty compost. The container can be left out for much of the year Up Country as long as it is protected during the coldest months.

Another established Cornish favourite, *C. sabatius*

C. cneorum in its glory, tumbling over a sunny wall

(formerly *C. mauritanicus*), is often sold as a patio plant for summer containers and treated by many gardeners as an annual. In fact it does have a perennial root system but is not invasive like its pesky cousin bindweed. The spreading, scrambling growth looks lovely when cascading over walls and can be seen to great effect by the bottom pool at Lamorran. Attractive blue flowers appear through summer into the autumn against contrasting matt green foliage.

C. Sabatius is often lost because it is too immature to survive its first winter. However, if it is kept away from frost and replanted in the second spring, it should by the autumn be tough enough to be left outdoors permanently, given sunshine and good drainage. Cut out fading shoots to encourage new ones from the roots. In colder parts in can be grown in a warm spot, if cut back in early winter and mulched for frost protection.

When not in flower, the foliage of *C. cneorum* can be used as a 'silver foil' for other elements in the garden. Here it contrasts well with the purple *Aeonium arboreum* and phormium, and a 'Titchmarsh Blue' shed

Salvia

Although somewhat tender, the late-flowering *Salvia leucantha* (Mexican sage) provides a much-coveted autumn display

The common herb sage (*Salvia officinalis*) has been popular in gardens and kitchens for centuries. There are many other salvias from different parts of the world, mostly South America, though few are hardy in the colder parts of England. Cornwall's mild winter climate, however, allows us to grow a wide range featuring some wonderfully-coloured flowers and a variety of leaf scents. Some have a pleasant odour, others quite the opposite. Most types are sub-shrubs in that they form a twiggy base which may survive the winter. Depending on the severity of the frost, many salvias will regenerate from their roots in spring after being cut to the ground, but others may be lost. There are scores from which to choose and it is easy to become hooked by their many charms. Here's a selection to whet your appetite.

The bushy *Salvia elegans* (pineapple sage) produces small red flowers in summer and autumn, its crushed leaves smelling attractively of pineapple. *S. leucantha* (Mexican sage) has woolly-textured white and violet flowers over dark green leaves. It is a favourite of Tim's mum Wendy, who likes to cut it for the house. It needs very good drainage. Two splendid taller-flowering types are *S.* 'Indigo Spires' (violet blue) and *S. uliginosa* (azure blue). The slender spikes of both look well with cannas. A new hybrid is *S.* 'Raspberry Royale', which displays an abundance of sumptuous red flowers over a long season on a compact bush. *S. confertiflora* is one of the sages whose leaves are unpleasant when crushed. However, its lovely foliage and slender vermilion-orange spikes in September-November make up for this. *S. microphylla* 'Trelissick' is one of the 'Eclipse' series

A varied gathering of salvias *S. involucrata, S. confertiflora, S. microphylla* with the blue *S. cacaliifolia* (Roy Cheek)

S. microphylla 'Trewithen Cerise' is one of the 'Eclipse' series introduced in 1999 (Kernock Park Plants)

introduced by Richard Harnett of Kernock Park Plants of Pillaton, Saltash, one of the country's biggest wholesale bedding plant producers. Its creamy yellow flowers are unusual in salvias. The microphyllas do in fact have a wide colour range and are fairly hardy, even Up Country.

If grown in pots on the patio, salvias can be brought into the conservatory in autumn to continue flowering, after which they should be kept dryish and frost free. If they are to be planted in the garden, take soft cuttings as insurance against losses from winter cold. Mulching the roots will help protect them from frost. When positioning salvias, bear in mind that they relish a Mediterranean-style climate of heat and a well-drained soil. To encourage sturdy new growth, cut the top hard back in spring, retaining the base of last year's growth. Dead-heading flower spikes will encourage more to grow from side shoots further down the stem.

Sun-loving Daisies

A wide range of free-flowering daisies from hot, dry climes brightens the Cornish garden scene. Most will close their flowers at night or in dull weather, a mechanism which protects them from being damaged by rain. Flowering can be all year round given favourable winters, though some types like to take a blooming holiday during summer. Most are available as bedding or patio plants and the various new or different types are always worth a try in Cornish gardens. They are ideal for bulking up new schemes while longer-term plants become established. The following selections chosen by Tim – though mostly short-lived – are all easily grown from cuttings.

Argyranthemum (Marguerite Daisy)

Most types of argyranthemum are from the Canary Islands and Madeira. They are very popular patio plants throughout the UK. Many new varieties are now becoming available and should be tried in Cornwall. The white-flowered marguerite is a long-established favourite, as is the vigorous yellow type 'Jamaica Primrose.' Most have green or grey-green leaves, and a fairly upright habit. They will develop a woody framework over the years, reaching up to two metres (seven feet) high.

Osteospermum (African Daisy)

These relatively new additions to the UK gardening scene are now widely planted in Cornwall. Most osteospermums have a low spreading habit and flower most profusely in spring and early summer. The flowers are usually white, pink or mauve. In recent years many new types in strong purples and yellows have been raised for annual bedding but as Cornish plants, most seem to lack hardiness or

Argyranthemum 'Jamaica Primrose' remains the best yellow-flowered marguerite daisy for perennial planting in Cornwall

The strong-growing arctotis (Zulu Daisy) oozes sunshine and gaiety over a long season (Kernock Park Plants)

durability to overwinter. Some varieties have contrasting undersides to the petals, which are attractive in themselves when the flowers close. Among the types known to be fairly hardy Up Country is *O.* 'Lady Leitrim'.

Arctotis (Zulu Daisy or Sunshine Flower)
These huge, jolly-looking daisies from South Africa are borne on long stalks. There is a range of flamboyant colours, including yellows, oranges and reds. Each giant bloom seems evocative of the sunshine and beauty of their native land. They have a tough, woolly, silvery foliage and are vigorous spreaders, providing excellent ground cover and growing to around 45 cms (18 inches) high. They can be seen along the sloping banks of Falmouth seafront on a large scale.

Osteospermum 'Whirlygig' is not the hardiest of African daisies, though its distinctive propeller-shaped petals make it a great favourite

More Sun-loving Daisies

Seen here with blue echium, the euryops (golden daisy bush) is seldom without flower in Cornwall

Felicia (Blue Marguerite)
This spreading, shrubby daisy from South Africa is less often seen than the others featured here but deserves to be more widely planted. It is distinguished by its delicate, two cm (¾ in) wide yellow-eyed sky-blue flowers on long stalks. White and extra-large blue flowered forms are also available.

Euryops (Golden Daisy Bush)
Another South African type, euryops is the shrubbiest of these daisies, quickly growing to one and a half metres (five feet). *E. pectinatus* makes an attractive grey-green foliage plant which contrasts well with the bright yellow flowers produced mainly in spring and then again through the winter. *E. chrysanthemoides* (often confused with argyranthemum) flowers freely from spring onwards.

Gazania (Treasure Flower)
Popularly known as the treasure flower in its native South Africa, and in Tim's view the most striking of all these daisies. Some gardeners find the dazzling hues of orange and yellow a little too strong for their tastes. Foliage ranges from green to silver. They form slowly-spreading clumps to 30 cms (one foot) high, their compact habit and bright colours making them good companions for the likes of yucca, puya and agave in the arid landscape. Good results can also be achieved annually from seed. Gazanias are especially popular in private gardens along the promenade at Penzance.

Erigeron
Two types are widely seen in Cornwall and often self-seed. *E. glaucus*, also known as seaside daisy or beach aster, comes from the coasts of California

The outstanding vibrant pink of *Gazania* 'Christopher Lloyd', an unusual colour in the range of treasure flowers (Kernock Park Plants)

and Oregon and has naturalised on some stretches of cliff in Cornwall. It enjoys the seaside but dislikes too much heat. Slowly spreading mats come to prominence in spring and summer, when the pale mauve daisies with large yellow centres look lovely growing in and over walls. *E. karvinskianus* (Mexican or Santa Barbara daisy) has flowers like the common lawn daisy, opening pink and changing to white over a long period. It readily seeds itself in walls, paths and steps and is very effective en masse. It is fairly hardy Up Country.

All these daisies will benefit from regular dead-heading. They love a dry, sunny bank, and soil with good winter drainage. Ideally, plant in spring and keep well watered until established. Hardiness varies greatly between the types so look for successes in other gardens and experiment in your own. Most have a reasonable tolerance to salt winds but don't enjoy cold blasts. Spring is a good time for trimming back established plants.

Erigeron karvinskianus (the Mexican or Santa Barbara daisy) is so often taken for granted, yet is one of the most durable and effective plants for difficult sites

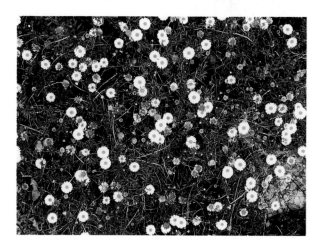

Good Gardens to Visit

Some of the gardens in Cornwall, Devon and beyond which have inspired the authors

Abbotsbury Sub Tropical gardens, near Weymouth
Antony, Torpoint
Arlington Court, near Barnstaple
Bicton Park, East Budleigh
Bosvigo, Truro
Caerhays Castle, Gorran
Carclew, Mylor
Carwinion, Mawnan Smith
Castle Drogo, Drewsteignton
Chyverton, Zelah
Coleton Fishacre, Kingswear
Cotehele, St Dominick
Cotswold Wildlife Park and Gardens, Burford
The Eden Project, Bodelva
Fox Rosehill, Falmouth
Glendurgan, Mawnan Smith
Headland, Polruan
Killerton, Broadclyst, Exeter
Knightshayes Court, Tiverton
Lamorran House, St Mawes
Lanhydrock, Bodmin
Lost Gardens of Heligan, Pentewan
Marwood Hill, Barnstaple
Mount Edgcumbe, Torpoint
Overbecks Museum and Garden, Salcombe
Paignton Zoo
Paradise Park, Hayle
Pencarrow, Bodmin
Penjerrick, Budock Water
Pine Lodge, St Austell
Probus, Truro
Queen Mary, Falmouth
RHS Garden, Rosemoor, Great Torrington
St Just-in-Roseland Church
St Michael's Mount, Marazion
The Garden House, Buckland Monachorum

Trebah, Mawnan Smith
Tregenna Castle, St Ives
Trelissick, Feock
Trengwainton, Penzance
Trerice, Newquay
Tresco Abbey, Isles of Scilly
Trevarno Estate, Helston
Trewidden, Penzance
Trewithen Gardens, Grampound Road

One of our favourite gardens – Fox Rosehill in its early spring glory

Nurseries

The king protea is a an iconic New Cornish Garden plant

ASHWOOD NURSERIES LIMITED – Fantastic salvias
Ashwood Lower Lane, Ashwood, Kingswinford, West Midlands. DY6 OAE
Tel: 01384 401996 web: www.ashwood-nurseries.co.uk

AVON BULBS – Superb range of bulbous plants
Burnt House Farm, Mid Lambrook, South Petherton, Somerset. TA13 5HE
Tel: 01460 242177 web: www.avonbulbs.com

BURNCOOSE NURSERIES – Extensive range of all sorts, many rare and unusual
Gwennap, Redruth, Cornwall. TR16 6BJ
Tel: 01209 860316 web: www.burncoose.co.uk

CHURCHTOWN NURSERIES
Shrubs, tender perennials, grasses
Gulval, Penzance, Cornwall. TR18 3BE
Tel: 01736 362626

CROSS COMMON NURSERY
Range of unusual tender plants for the seaside
Lizard Village, Helston, Cornwall. TR12 7PD
Tel: 01326 290722

DEVON AND DORSET BAMBOO
Bamboo specialist
Office: 13 Morley Road, Exeter, Devon. EX4 7BD
Tel: 01392 422853 web: www.devondorsetbamboo.com

DUCHY OF CORNWALL – Very wide range of plants
Penlyn Nursery, Cott Road, Lostwithiel, Cornwall. PL22 0HW
Tel: 01208 872668 web: www.duchyofcornwallnursery.co.uk

ENDSLEIGH GARDEN AND LEISURE – Extensive range
Ivybridge, Devon. PL21 9JL
Tel: 01752 898989

EUCALYPTUS NURSERIES
Specialists in hardy eucalyptus and some acacias
Carrog, Corwen, Denbighshire. LL21 9LD
Tel: 01490 430671

FIR TREE FARM NURSERY – Huge range of unusual plants
Tresahor, Constantine, Falmouth, Cornwall. TR11 5PL
Tel: 01326 340593 web: cornwallgardens.com

HARDY EXOTICS – Extensive jungle and arid plants
Gilly Lane Whitecross, Penzance, Cornwall. TR20 8BZ
Tel: 01736 740660 web: www.hardyexotics.co.uk

KOBAKOBA – Extensive range of bananas and gingers
Office: 2 High Street, Ashcott, Bridgwater, Somerset. TA7 9PL
Tel: 01458 210700 web: www.kobakoba.co.uk

LOWER KENNEGGY NURSERIES
Good range of succulents and southern hemisphere plants
Lower Kenneggy, Rosudgeon, Penzance, Cornwall. TR20 9AR
Tel: 01736 762959

The fine foliage and flowers of *Fuchsia* 'Thalia'

MARWOOD HILL GARDENS
Eucalyptus, camellia, bog plants
Barnstaple, Devon. EX31 4EB
Tel: 01271 342528

MULU NURSERIES
Bananas, ginger and canna lilies and other exotics
Longdon Hill, Wickhamford, Evesham, Worcs. WR11 7RP
Tel: 01386 833171 web: www.mulu.co.uk

OAKLAND NURSERIES
Large selection of abutilons, canna and ginger lilies, sun-loving daisies
147 Melton Road, Burton-on-the-Wolds, Loughborough, Leicestershire. LE12 5TQ
Tel: 01509 880646 web: www.oaklandnurseries.co.uk

PINE COTTAGE PLANTS
National collection of agapanthus
Fourways, Eggesford, Chulmleigh, Devon. EX18 7QZ
Tel: 01769 580076 Email: pcplants@mycabin.com

ROSELAND HOUSE NURSERY – Wide range of climbers and herbaceous plants
Chacewater, Truro, Cornwall. TR4 8QB
Tel: 01872 560451 web: www.roselandhouse.co.uk

SILVER DALE NURSERIES
National collection of fuchsia
Shute Lane, Combe Martin, Devon. EX34 OHT
Tel: 01271 882539 Email: silverdale.nurseries@virgin.net

SPECIAL PLANTS
Salvia, felicia, pelargonium
Greenways Lane, Cold Ashton, Chippenham, Wilts. SN14 8LA
Tel: 01225 891686 web: www.specialplants.net

THE PALM CENTRE
Extensive range of palms to try in Cornwall
Ham Central Nursery, Ham Street, Ham, Richmond. TW10 7HA
Tel: 0208 2556191 web: www.palmcentre.co.uk

TOWAN CAMELLIAS
Camellias big and small
John Price C/o Carwinion Gardens, Mawnan Smith, Falmouth, Cornwall. TR11 5JA
Te:l 01326 251115 By appointment

TRESSIDER FARM PLANTS – Protea family and succulents are specialities – by appointment
St. Buryan, Penzance, Cornwall. TR19 6EZ
Tel: 01736 810656

TREVENA CROSS NURSERIES – Exciting range of exotics including succulents, protea family and restios
Breage, Helston, Cornwall. TR13 9PS
Tel: 01736 763880 web: www.trevenacross.co.uk

TREWITHEN NURSERIES – Wide range of shrubs especially camellia and rhododendron
Grampound Road, Truro, Cornwall. TR2 4DD
Tel: 01726 882764

Pieris formosana displays its attractive new growths
(Clethra Matthews)

Bibliography

Arnold-Forster W., *Shrubs For The Milder Counties*
Alison Hodge
Bean W.J., *Trees And Shrubs Hardy In The British Isles*
(Eighth Edition) John Murray
The Hillier Manual of Trees & Shrubs (sixth edition)
David & Charles
Bell Michael, *The Gardener's Guide to Growing Temperate
Bamboos* David & Charles
Campbell-Culver Maggie, *The Origin of Plants* Headline
Cooke Ian, *The Plantfinder's Guide To Tender Perennials*
David & Charles
Davis Brian, *The Gardener's Illustrated Encyclopaedia of
Trees and Shrubs* Viking
Lord Tony, (Ed.) *R.H.S. Plant Finder* Dorling Kindersley
Pett Douglas Ellory, *The Cornwall Gardens Guide*
Alison Hodge
Pring Sue, (Ed.) *The Glorious Gardens of Cornwall*
Cornwall Gardens Trust
Thomas Graham Stuart, *Perennial Garden Plants* (third
Edition) Dent
Thurston Edgar, *British & Foreign Trees And Shrubs In
Cornwall* Cambridge University Press
Treseder Neil G., *Magnolias* Faber
Wray Nick, *Grow Something Different* BBC

Plant Vital Statistics & Botanical Index

The following table provides information to help you chose the right plants for your garden and to grow them well. This guide should be used in conjunction with Tim's Guide to Planting (pp 9-13). Remember, you need to develop an adventurous streak to be a true Cornish gardener. Plants often surprise us with their durability and versatility, so don't feel too constrained by our guidelines. Many thanks to Tim's good friend and mentor Roy Cheek for his help in developing the table. Together we have devised a grading system for the headings. In some cases it would be misleading to give a single grade, so more than one appears – eg C&B. Use of a hyphen eg C-A, indicates a wide range, with a slight preference for the first grade, C. Where two grades appear together, eg AB, this means the preference lies between A and B.

The growth guide refers to plants taken from the most common size available, usually two or three litre pots, and planted in the preferred conditions as outlined. Dimensions include flower spikes.

Key to grades:

Frost Hardiness
- A Hardy in much of Britain
- B Hardy in Cornwall/sheltered spots in much of Britain
- C Hardy in much of Cornwall/sheltered spots in warmer areas
- D Tolerant of light frosts

Soil Drainage
- A Extremely well drained
- B Well drained but retaining some moisture in summer
- C Retains good levels of moisture during summer but not water-logged in winter
- D Wet for most of year

Soil pH Guide
- A Acid
- B Slightly acid to neutral provided it doesn't dry out
- C Mildly alkaline soils tolerated

Cold Wind Tolerance
- A very
- B fairly
- C Not very

Salt Wind Tolerance
- A Very
- B Fairly
- C Not very

Light Preference (Sun/Shade)
- A Shade
- B Sunny position if soil doesn't dry out
- C Full sun

Plant list and growing conditions / habit assessment

Plant name	Page no	Frost hardiness	Soil drainage	Soil pH	Cold wind tolerance	Salt wind tolerance	Sun / shade	Growth guide ht x spread		
								2 years	5 years	10 years
Abutilon 'Golden Fleece'	50	DC	B&C	C	C	BC	CA	1.5 x 1.0	2.0 x 1.8	2.4 x 2.2
megapotamicum	50	B	B&C	C	C	B	BA	1.0 x 0.6	2.0 x 0.8	3.0 x 1.0
ochsenii	50	B	B&C	C	C	B	BC	1.5 x 0.8	3.0 x 1.5	4.0 x 2.0
'Patrick Synge'	50	B	B	C	C	CB	C-A	2.0 x 1.1	3.0 x 2.0	3.5 x 4.0
x suntense 'Jermyns'	51	B	B&C	C	C	B	B&C	2.0 x 1.0	4.5 x 2.0	6.0 x 4.0
vitifolium 'Album'	51	B	B&C	C	C	B	B&C	1.8 x 0.9	4.0 x 1.8	5.0 x 3.0
Acacia dealbata	40	BC	B	BC	C	B	C	2.5 x 1	5.0 x 3.0	2.5 x 1.0
dealbata subalpina	40	B	B	C	C	B	C	2.0 x 1.0	4.0 x 3.0	9.0 x 5.0
pravissima	40	B	B	CB	CB	BA	C	1.2 x 1.0	2.0 x 2.0	4.0 x 3.0
verticillata	41	DC	B	BC	C	BA	C	1.4 x 1.7	2.1 x 1.1	4.2 x 2.1
Aeonium arboreum & varieties	107	D	A	C	C	BA	C	0.7 X 0.4	1.0 X 0.9	*
Agapanthus Headbourne hybrids	70	A	B	C	B	B	C	0.6 x 0.5	0.7 x 0.9	0.7 x 1.3
'Jack's Blue'	70	A	B	C	B	B	C	1.0 x 0.6	1.5 x 1.0	1.6 x 1.6
'Rosewarne'	70	C	A&B	C	C	B	C	0.9 x 0.6	1.0 x 1.2	1.0 x 2.0
Agave americana	88	B	A&B	C	C	A	C	0.8 x 0.8	1.5 x 1.5	2.0 x 2.0
'Variegata'	89	CB	A&B	C	C	A	C	0.6 x 0.6	1.2 x 1.2	1.5 x 1.5
celsii	89	D	A&B	C	C	BA	C	0.4 x 0.4	0.6 x 0.7	2.2 x 1.3
ferox	88	BC	A&B	C	C	A	C	0.3 x 0.4	0.7 x 0.8	1.0 x 1.2
Amaryllis belladonna	78	B	B&C	C	C	B	C	0.6 x 0.3	0.6 x 0.4	0.6 x 0.6
Araucaria araucana	62	A	C	C	B	A	A-C	0.6 x 0.6	1.0 x 0.9	2.0 x 1.2
heterophylla	63	D	B	C	C	CB	C	0.9 x 0.6	1.6 x 1.2	5.0 x 3.0
Arctotis	111	BC	A&B	C	C	B	C	0.3 X 1.8	0.4 X 4.0	*
Argyranthemum (White Marguerite)	110	C	B&A	C	C	B	C	0.9 x 0.9	1.5 x 1.5	0.9 x 2.0
'Jamaica Primrose'	110	C	B&A	C	C	B	C	0.8 x 0.9	1.5 x 1.5	*
Arundo donax	67	A	B-D	C	B	A	C	2.0 x 0.8	3.1 x 1.4	4.0 x 2.1
'Macrophylla'	67	A	B-D	C	B	A	C	2.0 x 0.8	3.1 x 1.4	4.0 x 2.1
'Variegata'	67	C	B&C	C	C	A	C	1.8 x 0.6	2.0 x 1.5	2.2 x 1.1
Beschorneria yuccoides	92	B	A&B	C	C	BA	C	0.6 x 0.6	3.0 x 2.0	3.0 x 3.0
Butia capitata	85	B	B	C	C	CB	C	1.0 x 0.7	1.5 x 1.0	2.0 x 2.0
Callistemon citrinus & varieties	44	C	A-C	BC	C	AB	C	0.9 x 0.6	1.5 x 1.2	2.0 x 2.0
ridgidus	45	B	A-C	BC	CB	A	C	1.2 x 1.0	1.8 x 1.5	2.1 x 2.5
salignus	45	B	A-C	BC	CB	AB	C	1.2. X 1.0	1.8 x 1.5	2.1 x 2.5
sieberi	45	A	A-C	BC	B	AB	C	0.6 x 4.0	1.2 x 0.9	1.6 x 0.9

Plant name	Page no	Frost hardiness	Soil drainage	Soil pH	Cold wind tolerance	Salt wind tolerance	Sun / shade	Growth guide ht x spread		
								2 years	5 years	10 years
Camellia japonica	16	A	C	A&B	B	B	BA	0.8 X 0.4	1.5 x 0.7	2.2 x 1.8
saluenensis	16	C	C	A&B	C	B	BA	0.7 X 0.4	1.3 x 0.6	1.8 x 1.5
x williamsii 'St Ewe'	16	A	C	A&B	AB	BA	BA	0.9 X 0.5	1.8 x 0.7	3.0 x 2.0
Canna 'Durban'	75	C	B	C	C	BC	C&B	1.0 x 0.6	0.3 x 0.8	1.3 x 1.0
indica	75	B	B	C	CB	B	C	1.8 x 0.6	2.0 x 0.9	2.0 x 1.3
iridiflora	75	B	B	C	CB	B	C&B	1.0 x 0.7	1.2 x 1.2	1.2 x 1.2
'Panache'	75	B	B	C	CB	B	B&C	1.0 x 0.5	1.5 x 0.7	1.5 x 0.9
'Wyoming'	75	B	B	C	B	B	C	1.6 x 0.6	1.8 x 0.9	1.8 x 1.3
Carpenteria californica	48	A	C	C	BC	B	C	0.9 x 0.8	1.2 x 1.0	2.0 x 1.6
Carpobrotus edulis	98	C	A	C	C	A	C	0.1 x 1.5	0.2 x 3.0	0.2 x 6.0
Cautleya spicata 'Robusta'	72	B	BC	C	C	CB	C-A	0.6 x 0.4	0.9 x 0.9	0.9 x 1.2
Chamaerops humilis	82	B	A&B	C	C	AB	C-A	0.7 x 0.6	0.9 x 0.9	1.5 x 1.5
Chionochloa conspicua	66	BA	B&C	B	C	BC	A&B	1.2 x 0.7	1.8 x 0.9	1.8 x 1.0
Chusquea culeou	64	A	C	BC	B	C	BA	1.4 x 0.8	1.7 x 0.8	3.0 x 2.0
Clianthus puniceus	54	C	B	CB	C	B	C	1.6 x 1.6	2.0 x 2.0	2.6 x 3.0
puniceus 'Kaka King'	55	B	B	CB	C	B	C	1.6 x 1.6	2.0 x 2.0	2.6 x 3.0
Convolvulus cneorum	106	B	B	C	C	BA	C	0.4 x 0.7	0.6 x 0.8	0.7 x 1.0
sabatius	106	B	B	C	C	B	C	0.2 x 0.6	0.2 x 0.8	0.2 x 1.0
Cordyline australis	80	B	BC	C	CB	A	C	1.2 x 0.9	3.0 x 1.6	5.0 x 2.0
'Red Star' & 'Torbay Red'	81	B	BC	C	C	BA	C	0.9 X 0.7	2.0 X 1.2	3.5 X 1.5
'Torbay Dazzler'	81	DC	BC	C	C	B	C	0.8 x 0.7	1.5 x 1.0	2.8 x 1.2
'Variegata'	81	DC	BC	C	C	B	C	0.8 x 0.7	1.4 x 1.0	2.6 x 1.2
indivisa	81	C	C	C	C	B	AB	0.3 x 0.3	1.6 x 1.3	3.0 x 1.6
Cortaderia richardii	66	BA	B	BC	BC	B	C	0.9 x 1.0	1.8 x 1.5	2.1 x 1.6
selloana	66	A	C-A	C	B	A	C	1.8 x 1.0	2.5 x 2.0	2.8 x 3.0
'Pumila'	66	A	C-A	C	BC	A	C	1.8 x 1.6	2.0 x 2.0	2.0 x 3.0
Crinodendron hookerianum	22	B	C	B	C	B	BA	0.9 x 0.7	1.6 x 1.0	2.6 x 1.5
Crocosmia x crocosmiiflora	76	A	B&C	C	B	B	C-A	0.6 x 0.4	0.6 x 0.9	0.6 x 1.2
'Carmin Brilliant'	77	A	B&C	C	B	BC	C	0.7 x 0.4	0.7 x 0.9	0.7 x 1.2
'Solfatare'	77	B	B&C	C	C	BC	C	0.6 x 0.5	0.7 x 0.9	0.7 x 1.3
Cupressus macrocarpa	42	A	BC	C	B	A	C	1.2 x 0.5	1.8 x 0.8	3.2 x 2.0
'Goldcrest'	43	A	BC	C	B	A	C	1.1 x 0.5	1.8 x 0.8	3.5 x 1.8
Crinum bulbispermum	78	C	B	C	C	C	C-A	1.0 x 0.5	1.2 x 0.7	1.2 x 1.2

Plant list and growing conditions / habit assessment

Plant name	Page no	Frost hardiness	Soil drainage	Soil pH	Cold wind tolerance	Salt wind tolerance	Sun / shade	Growth guide ht x spread		
								2 years	5 years	10 years
moorei	78	C	B	C	C	C	C	1.0 x 0.5	1.2 x 0.6	1.2 x 1.0
x powellii	78	CB	BC	C	C	B	C	1.0 x 0.5	1.2 x 0.6	1.2 x 1.0
Cyathea dealbata	57	D	C	CB	C	C	A	height increase 0.6m per 10 yrs		
medullaris	57	D	C	CB	C	C	AB	height increase 0.6m per 10 yrs		
Dendromecon rigida	48	BC	B	BC	C	CB	C	0.6 x 0.3	1.2 x 0.6	1.8 x 1.8
Dicksonia antarctica	56	AB	B-D	C	C	C	A&B	height increase 0.3 m per 10 yrs		
Echium pininana	104	DC	B	C	C	BA	C	4.0 x 1.0	*	*
wildpretii	105	C	A	C	C	B	C	2.0 x 0.6	*.	*
Elaeagnus x ebbingei	9	A	C&B	C	A	A	C-A	0.9 x 0.8	1.3 x 1.3	2.1 x 2.1
Elegia cuspidata	69	B	B	C	C	B	C	1.4 x 0.8	2.0 x 1.0	2.0 x 1.5
Embothrium lanceolatum	24	BA	C	B	C	C	B	1.5 x 0.5	2.6 x 1.0	5.0 x 3.0
lanceolatum 'Norquinco'	24	A	C	B	B	BC	B	1.5 x 0.5	2.6 x 1.0	5.0 x 3.0
longifolium	24	B	C	B	C	C	B	1.5 x 0.6	2.8 x 1.0	6.0 x 3.0
Ensete ventricosum	61	D	B&C	C	C	C	C	1.8 x 1.8	3.0 x 3.0	4.5 x 4.0
Erigeron glaucus	112	C	B	C	C	A	C	0.1 x 0.6	0.2 x 0.8	0.2 x 1.2
karvinskianus	113	A	A&B	C	A	A	C	0.2 x 0.3	0.2 x 0.4	*
Erythrina crista-galli	52	B	B	C	C	B	C	0.9 x 0.7	1.6 x 1.2	2.0 x 2.0
Erythrina c-g 'Compacta'	53	DC	B	C	C	B	C	0.5 x 0.4	0.7 x 0.8	0.9 x 0.9
Escallonia rubra macrantha	9	BC	A-C	BC	CB	A	CA	1.1 x 0.9	2.2 x 1.8	3.3 x 4.0
Eucalyptus ficifolia	38	D	B	B	C	B	C	1.5 x 0.9	3.5 x 2.0	7.0 x 3.-0
niphophila	39	A	BC	B	A	A	C	1.6 x 1.0	4.0 x 2.0	9.0 x 4.0
pauciflora	39	A	BC	B	BA	A	C	2.0 x 1.0	6.0 x 3.0	12 x 5.0
Euryops chrysanthemoides	112	C	B	C	C	B	C	1.0 x 1.2	1.7 x 2.2	*
pectinatus	112	C	B	C	C	B	C	0.9 x 1.0	1.7 x 2.0	*
Fargesia nitida	65	A	C	C	BA	BA	AB	1.4 x 0.5	2.1 x 1.1	3.0 x 2.2
Fascicularia bicolor	94	B	A	C	BC	A	A-C	0.2 x 0.3	0.3 x 0.6	0.4 x 1.0
Felicia amelloides	112	CB	B	C	C	AB	C	0.2 x 0.6	0.3 x 1.0	*
Fuchsia 'Genii'	87	A	BC	C	BA	BA	B-A	0.7 x 0.5	1.0 x 0.8	1.4 x 0.9
magellanica molinae	28	A	C	C	AB	A	BA	1.0 x 0.9	1.8 x 1.5	2.5 x 1.7
magellenica 'Riccartonii'	28	A	CB	C	B	A	B-A	1.0 x 0.9	2.0 x 1.6	3.0 x 1.8
'Mrs Popple'	28	A	CB	C	B	BA	B-A	0.8 x 0.6	1.1 x 0.8	1.4 x 1.5
procumbens	29	D	C	C	C	C	B	0.1 x 0.6	0.1 x 1.0	0.1 x 1.2
splendens	28	D	C	C	C	CB	B-A	0.6 x 0.5	0.9 x 0.7	1.0 x 0.9

Plant name	Page no	Frost hardiness	Soil drainage	Soil pH	Cold wind tolerance	Salt wind tolerance	Sun / shade	Growth guide ht x spread		
								2 years	5 years	10 years
'Thalia'	29	D	B	C	C	B	C-A	0.9 x 0.6	1.2 x 0.8	1.4 x 0.9
Gazania varieties	112	B	A&B	C	C	AB	C	0.3 x 0.4	0.3 x 0.6	*
Geranium maderense	102	DC	B	C	C	B	A	0.9 x 1.0	*	*
palmatum	103	DC	B	C	C	B	A	0.9 x 1.0	*	*
Griselinia littoralis	9	C	B&C	C	C	A	C-A	1.3 x 0.8	2.0 x 1.7	3.4 x 2.0
'Bantry Bay'	9	D	B&C	C	C	BA	C&B	0.6 x 0.4	1.1 x 0.6	1.6 x 1.1
Gunnera manicata	58	A	D	C	C	B	B&A	0.9 x 0.9	1.5 x 1.5	3.0 x 3.0
tinctoria	59	A	D	C	C	B	B&A	0.7 x 0.7	1.2 x 1.2	1.8 x 1.8
Hebe x andersonii	32	CB	B	C	CB	AB	CA	1.0 x 0.4	1.5 x 1.0	2.0 x 1.5
'Variegata'	32	C	B	C	C	BA	C	0.3 x 0.3	1.2 x 0.9	1.6 x 1.3
x franciscana 'Blue Gem'	32	B	B	C	BC	A	C	0.6 x 0.6	0.9 x 1.1	1.4 x 2.0
'Variegata'	32	BC	B	C	CB	AB	C	0.5 x 0.5	0.7 x 0.8	1.1 x 1.8
'Great Orme'	32	B	B	C	C	B	C	0.7 x 0.8	1.0 x 1.2	1.4 x 1.8
'Red Edge'	33	A	B	C	BA	AB	CA	0.3 x 0.5	0.5 x 0.9	0.5 x 1.0
salicifolia	33	A	B	C	BC	BA	C	0.8 x 0.8	1.2 x 1.2	1.6 x 1.6
'Simon Delaux'	32	B	B	C	C	B	C	0.7 x 0.8	1.0 x 1.2	1.4 x 1.8
Hedychium coccineum 'Tara'	72	A	CB	C	C	CB	B	1.0 x 0.4	1.6 x 0.8	1.8 x 1.0
gardnerianum	72	C	CB	C	C	CB	B	0.8 x 0.5	0.9 x 0.8	1.0 x 1.0
'Great Dixter'	72	C	CB	C	C	CB	B	0.8 x 0.5	0.9 x 0.8	1.2 x 1.0
'Pink V'	73	C	B&C	C	C	BC	B	1.2 x 0.4	1.2 x 0.7	1.5 x 0.9
Hydrangea macrophylla varieties	26	A	C&B	A-C	BC	AB	BA	0.9 x 0.8	1.6 x 1.8	2.2 x 3.0
'Sea Foam'	27	CB	C&B	A-C	C	AB	BA	0.9 x 0.8	1.6 x 1.8	2.0 x 2.0
Lonicera hildebrandiana	13	D	B	C	C	C	CB	1.8 x 1.0	3.0 x 2.0	4.0 x 4.0
Magnolia 'Caerhays Belle'	14	A	C	A&B	C	C	B	1.3 x 1.2	2.2 x 2.0	3.0 x 2.7
campbellii	14	A	C	A&B	CB	BA	B	1.4 x 1.2	3.0 x 2.5	5.0 x 4.0
x loebneri 'Leonard Messel'	15	A	C&B	C	B	CB	B	1.4 x 1.2	2.2 x 2.2	4.0 x 3.0
'Merrill'	15	A	C&B	C	B	CB	B	1.3 x 1.1	2.0 x 2.0	3.5 x 2.5
sargentiana robusta	14	A	C	A&B	C	C	B	1.3 x 1.2	2.2 x 2.0	3.0 x 2.5
sprengeri diva	14	A	C	A&B	C	C	B	1.3 x 0.7	2.1 x 1.2	3.5 x 3.0
'Star Wars'	14	A	C	A&B	C	C	B	1.2 x 0.6	2.0 x 1.0	3.2 x 2.8
stellata & varieties	15	A	C&B	C	B	CB	B	0.8 x 0.7	1.1 x 1.3	1.5 x 2.0
Mesembryanthemum	98	D	A	C	C	A	C	0.1 x 0.5	0.2 x 0.9	*
Musa basjoo	60	A	B&C	C	C	CB	B	2.0 x 2.4	4.0 x 4.0	4.0 x 5.0

Plant list and growing conditions / habit assessment

Plant name	Page no	Frost hardiness	Soil drainage	Soil pH	Cold wind tolerance	Salt wind tolerance	Sun / shade	Growth guide ht x spread		
								2 years	5 years	10 years
Myrtus communis	30	B	B	C	C	B	AC	0.9 x 0.9	1.5 x 1.5	2.2 x 2.0
tarentina	31	B	B	C	C	BA	AC	0.7 x 0.7	1.0 x 1.0	1.7 x 1.4
lechleriana	31	CB	C	BC	C	CB	AC	0.9 x 0.6	1.5 x 1.0	2.5 x 1.6
luma	30	BA	CB	B	C	B	AC	0.9 x 0.5	1.5 x 0.8	2.5 x 1.6
luma 'Penwith'	31	BC	CB	B	C	B	BC	0.7 x 0.4	1.2 x 0.6	1.8 x 1.2
Ochagavia rosea	95	B	A&B	C	C	AB	C	0.2 x 0.3	0.2 x 0.5	0.3 x 0.9
Olearia 'Henry Travers'	35	DC	B	C	C	B	C	0.9 x 1.0	1.5 x 1.7	2.5 x 2.5
macrodonta	35	A	B	C	B	BA	C	0.9 x 0.8	1.8 x 1.6	3.2 x 3.0
phlogopappa	35	BC	B	C	C	BC	C	0.9 x 1.0	1.5 x 1.7	2.5 x 2.5
x scilloniensis	34	C	B	C	C	AB	C	0.9 x 1.0	1.4 x1.6	1.9 x 2.3
traversii	35	D	B&A	C	C	A	C	1.8 x 0.9	3.5 x 1.8	5.0 x 2.7
x 'Zennorensis'	34	C	A&B	C	C	A	C	0.7 x 0.8	1.1 x 1.1	1.6 x 1.5
Osteospermum jucundum	110	C	A&B	C	C	BA	C	0.3 x 1.2	0.4 x 1.6	*
'Lady Leitrim'	111	BA	A&B	C	CB	BA	C	0.3 x 0.9	0.4 x 1.3	*
'Whirlygig'	111	D	A&B	C	C	B	CA	0.3 x 0.6	1.0 x 0.7	*
Pelargonium 'Amethyst' (ivy-leaved)	100	D	BA	C	C	BA	CA	1.4 x 1.2	3.0 x 3.0	4.0 x 4.0
'Caroline Schmidt' (zonal)	100	D	B	C	C	BA	CA	0.9 x 0.5	1.1 x 0.7	*
'Clorinda'	101	D	BA	C	C	BA	CA	1.2 x 0.9	2.5 x 1.8	*
'Graveolens'	100	DC	BA	C	C	BA	CA	0.5 x 0.9	0.6 x 1.2	*
'Lady Plymouth'	100	D	BA	C	C	BA	CA	0.6 x 0.7	0.9 x 0.9	*
papilionaceum	101	C	BC	B	C	C	AB	1.1 x 0.9	1.7 x 1.0	2.0 x 1.6
'Royal Oak'	100	C	BA	C	C	BA	CA	0.5 x 0.9	0.6 x 1.2	*
'Unique' types	100	CD	BA	C	C	AB	CA	0.5 x 0.4	0.4 x 0.7	*
Phoenix canariensis	84	CB	B	C	C	B	C	1.2 x 1.1	1.8 x 1.8	2.8 x 2.8
dactylifera	84	D	B	C	C	B	C	1.0 x 1.0	1.5 x 1.5	2.4 x 2.4
Phormium cookianum	86	B	C	C	C	AB	BC	0.5 x 0.9	0.8 x 1.3	1.1 x 2.0
tenax	86	A	C	C	C	A	A-C	0.6 x 0.7	1.0 x 1.1	1.9 x 1.8
Phyllostachys aureosulcata & types	65	A	C	CB	B	CB	c-a	2.1 x 1.2	3.2 x 1.8	4.0 x 2.5
bissetii	64	A	C	CB	A	AB	B	2.0 x 1.5	2.5 x 2.5	3.0 x 3.5
edulis	65	A	C	C	C	C	BA	1.3 x 0.8	2.0 x 1.2	4.0 x 2.2
nigra	64	A	C	CB	BC	C	B	1.4 x 0.9	2.5 x 1.8	3.2 x 2.3
vivax 'Aureocaulis'	65	A	C	CB	CB	CB	C-A	2.0 x 1.3	3.5 x 2.0	5.0 x 3.0

Plant name	Page no	Frost hardiness	Soil drainage	Soil pH	Cold wind tolerance	Salt wind tolerance	Sun / shade	Growth guide ht x spread		
								2 years	5 years	10 years
Pieris 'Bert Chandler'	21	AB	C	A	C	C	BA	0.6 x 0.6	0.9 x 0.9	1.3 x 1.3
'Forest Flame'	20	A	C	A	CB	C	AB	0.8 x 0.6	1.2 x 0.9	1.8 x 1.5
forrestii 'Charles Michael'	20	AB	C	A	C	C	AB	0.8 x 0.6	1.3 x 1.0	2.0 x 1.8
forrestii 'Wakehurst'	20	A	C	A	C	C	AB	0.7 x 0.5	1.0 x 0.8	1.4 x 1.1
japonica	20	A	C	A	C	C	AB	0.6 x 0.4	0.9 x 0.7	1.2 x 2.0
japonica 'Flaming Star'	20	BA	C	A	C	C	B	0.5 x 0.3	0.8 x 0.5	0.9 x 1.0
Pinus radiata	42	BA	BC	BC	BC	A	C	0.9 x 0.4	2.0 x 1.4	5.0 x 4.0
Pittosporum eugenioides	37	BC	B	C	C	B	C-A	1.1 x 0.6	2.0 x 1.4	4.0 x 2.8
'Garnettii'	36	B	B	C	C	A	C-A	0.9 x 0.4	1.6 x 0.9	3.0 x 2.0
tenuifolium	36	B	B	C	CB	A	C-A	1.1 x 0.5	2.0 x 1.1	4.0 x 2.5
'Elizabeth'	37	AB	B	C	CB	A	CA	0.9 x 0.4	1.6 x 0.9	3.0 x 2.0
'Green Elf'	37	AB	B	C	CB	A	CB	0.4 x 0.3	0.6 x 0.5	1.0 x 1.0
'James Stirling'	36	C	B	C	C	BA	CB	1.0 x 0.4	1.8 x 0.9	3.7 x 2.1
'Purpureum'	36	BC	B	C	C	BA	CB	0.9 x 0.4	1.4 x 0.8	2.6 x 1.6
'Silver Queen'	36	B	B	C	CB	A	C-A	0.8 x 0.3	1.6 x 0.8	2.6 x 1.6
'Tiki'	37	B	B	C	CB	A	CB	0.7 x 0.3	1.2 x 0.6	2.0 x 1.0
'Tom Thumb'	37	CB	B	C	C	BA	C&B	0.3 x 0.2	0.6 x 0.5	0.9 x 1.0
'Victoria'	37	AB	B	C	CB	AB	CA	1.1 x 0.6	1.6 x 0.9	2.0 x 1.5
'Warnham Gold'	36	C	B	C	C	BA	C&B	0.8 x 0.4	1.5 x 0.8	2.1 x 1.5
tobira	37	C	BA	C	C	A	C	0.6 x 0.8	1.1 x 1.4	2.0 x 1.6
Protea cynaroides	46	C	AB	A	C	AB	C	0.8 x 0.6	1.5 x 0.9	2.0 x 1.3
eximia	47	C	A&B	A-C	C	A	C	0.9 x 0.6	1.7 x 0.9	2.7 x 1.3
grandiceps	47	C	A	A	C	AB	C	0.5 x 0.6	0.8 x 0.9	1.6 x 1.8
neriifolia	11	DC	A&B	A	C	AB	C	0.5 x 0.6	0.7 x 1.2	0.9 x 2.0
subvestita	47	C	A	A	C	B	C	0.3 x 0.3	0.8 x 0.7	1.4 x 1.1
Pseudosasa japonica	64	A	C&B	C	AB	AB	A-C	1.3 x 0.4	2.0 x 1.0	3.0 x 2.0
Puya alpestris	96	A&b	A	C	C	A	C	0.4 x 0.4	0.4 x 0.5	1.3 x 0.8
chilensis	96	A&B	A	C	C	A	C	0.5 x 0.5	1.0 x 0.9	3.0 x 2.0
mirabilis	97	A&B	A	C	C	AB	C	0.2 x 0.2	0.3 x 0.3	0.8 x 0.5
Quercus ilex	9	A	B&C	C	B	A	A-C	0.5 x 0.3	1.2 x 0.6	2.8 x 0.9
Rhodocoma gigantea	69	B	B&C	B	C	BC	A&B	1.3 x 0.9	2.2 x 1.8	3.0 x 2.0
Rhododendron arboreum	18	B	C	A	cb	C	B-A	1.0 x 0.8	1.6 x 1.2	2.3 x 1.8
'Barclayi Robert Fox'	19	C	C	A	C	CB	A-B	0.9 x 0.7	1.3 x 0.9	2.1 x 1.7

Plant list and growing conditions / habit assessment

Plant name	Page no	Frost hardiness	Soil drainage	Soil pH	Cold wind tolerance	Salt wind tolerance	Sun / shade	Growth guide ht x spread		
								2 years	5 years	10 years
'Beauty of Tremough'	19	C	C	A	C	C	A-B	0.9 x 0.6	1.1 x 0.9	1.9 x 1.6
'Cornish Cross'	19	CB	C	A	C	C	A-B	0.7 x 0.6	1.4 x 0.9	2.3 x 1.8
luteum	19	A	C&B	A	CB	CB	A-B	0.7 x 0.7	1.1 x 1.1	2.1 x 2.0
'Penjerrick'	18	B	C	A	C	C	A-B	1.1 x 0.7	2.0 x 1.6	3.0 x 2.0
sinogrande	18	AB	C	A	C	C	A	0.9 x 0.8	1.6 x 1.4	2.3 x 2.5
ponticum	19	A	C&B	AB	BA	BA	A-C	1.0 x 0.8	1.9 x 1.3	2.5 x 1.9
'Sir Charles Lemon'	18	B	C	A	C	BC	B-A	1.0 x 0.8	1.6 x 1.2	2.3 x 1.8
Romneya coulteri	48	A	A-B	C	B	AB	C	0.6 x 0.8	1.5 x 1.2	2.0 x 1.8
Salvia cacaliifolia	109	D	A	C	C	CB	C	0.7 x 0.6	0.8 x 0.8	*
confertiflora	108	D	A	C	C	B	C	1.3 x 0.9	1.5 x 1.3	*
elegans	108	B	A	C	C	AB	C	1.0 x 0.9	1.2 x 1.3	1.3 x 1.6
'Indigo Spires'	108	B	A	C	C	C	C	1.7 x 0.5	1.8 x 0.8	*
involucrata	109	BA	AB	C	C	C	C	1.0 X 0.6	1.4 x 0.9	1.5 x 1.2
leucantha	108	D	A	C	C	B	C	0.7 x 1.0	1.0 x 1.6	*
microphylla 'Varieties'	108	B	A	C	BC	B	C	0.6 x 0.4	0.7 x 0.6	*
officinalis	108	A	B	C	BA	B	C	0.4 x 0.5	0.6 x 1.0	*
'Raspberry Royale'	108	B	A	C	C	B	C	0.7 x 0.5	0.8 x 0.7	*
uliginosa	108	AB	A	C	BC	BC	C	1.3 x 0.7	1.5 x 1.2	1.5 x 1.6
Senna corymbosa	53	CB	BC	C	C	B	C-A	1.0 x 1.0	2.2 x 3.0	3.0 x 4.0
Sophora microphylla 'Sun King'	54	A	BC	C	BC	B	C	0.8 x 0.5	1.2 x 0.9	2.0 x 1.4
tetraptera	54	B	BC	C	C	B	C	1.0 x 0.6	2.2 x 0.9	4.0 x 1.5
Thamnochortus lucens	69	CB	B	B	C	BC	C	0.5 x 0.4	0.6 x 0.6	0.6 x 0.8
Trachycarpus fortunei	82	A	B&C	C	CB	BC	A&B	0.7 x 0.7	1.0 x 1.0	2.0 x 1.8
Yucca aloifolia	90	B	A&B	C	C	A	C	1.0 x 0.7	1.6 x 1.2	3.0 x 2.0
'Variegata'	91	C	A&B	C	C	A	C	0.8 x 0.6	1.2 x 0.9	2.0 x 1.8
elephantipes	90	D	A&B	C	C	BA	A-C	0.9 x 0.7	1.2 x 0.9	2.1 x 1.0
gloriosa	91	A	A-C	C	B	A	A-C	0.8 x 0.7	1.1 x 0.9	2.0 x 1.4
recurvifolia	91	A	A-C	C	B	AB	A-C	0.9 x 0.6	1.3 x 0.7	2.0 x 1.2
whipplei	90	B	A&B	C	C	BA	C	0.3 x 0.4	4.0 x 0.5	*

Tim Miles   David Rowe

Tim Miles

Growing up in Falmouth, Tim Miles was deeply influenced by the range of exotic plants growing around the town, and by the comments of horticulturally-impressed visitors to his parents' guest house. From a young age, he appreciated that Cornwall was a special place to garden.

During this period, Falmouth was being championed, via the *Britain in Bloom* competition, by the legendary Don Hoyle. Later Don became the south-west's premier TV gardening celebrity and Tim appeared with him on the BBC's *According to Hoyle* series.

Tim studied at Cannington (under Roy Cheek) and Pershore Colleges and has since developed two notable private gardens (in Surrey and Hampshire) and those at London Zoo, each with a significant degree of Cornish influence. Tim's pioneering of the exotic style continues at the Cotswold Wildlife Park in Oxfordshire, which is fast becoming celebrated for its flamboyant gardens.

He was curator at Heligan and has also travelled widely to visit gardens. As a member of RHS floral committee C, he regularly judges at major flower shows such as Chelsea.

Tim lives in Burford with his wife Annette and two daughters. He represented Cornwall at rugby and is a keen cricketer and sailor.

David Rowe

David Rowe is a freelance journalist. He grew up in Cornwall, leaving to take a journalism course at Portsmouth. After training as a reporter on the *Devon and Somerset News*, he joined the *Falmouth Packet,* his home-town paper.

He left again to take a degree in English and Philosophy at the University of Kent at Canterbury. He was awarded a first and prize for best combined honours result in his faculty.

David became chief reporter of the *Kent Evening Post.* Then for nearly ten years he travelled Britain and the five continents as a Fleet Street staff features writer with *Today* and the *Sunday Mirror.* As a freelance he has written for many publications ranging from *Your Garden* to *The Guardian* to *Good Housekeeping.*

He came home to Cornwall in 1998 with Kathy and their two daughters. They soon added a third.

In his teens David played football to senior standard in Cornwall. Since coming back he has tried to play again. He also enjoys squash, and loves the coastal path and moors.

To his surprise since acquiring a garden, he has become mildly obsessed with Cornish planting generally - and mad about *Echium pininana.*